THE CITY OF LONDON

A Masonic Guide

Yasha Beresiner

Lewis Masonic

First published 2006
Reprinted 2011

ISBN 978 0 85318 254 2

All rights reserved. No part of this book
may be reproduced or transmitted in any
form or by any means, electronic or
mechanical, including photocopying,
recording or by any information storage
and retrieval system, without permission
from the Publisher in writing.

© Yasha Beresiner 2006

Published by Lewis Masonic

an imprint of Ian Allan Publishing Ltd,
Hersham, Surrey KT12 4RG.
Printed in England by Ian Allan Printing
Ltd, Hersham, Surrey KT12 4RG.

Code: 1108/A

Visit the Lewis Masonic website at
www.lewismasonic.com

Dedication
The new print of the book is dedicated,
at the start of the sixth decade of our
marriage, to Zmira with total love and
affection.

Picture Credits
Pictures reproduced in this book are
from the author's collection unless
otherwise credited. The abbreviated
credits are as follows: YB author;
LZ Leo Zanelli; DP David Peabody.

Front cover: Cheapside was the 'Oxford Street' of the olden days. DP

'Earth has not anything to show more fair:
Dull would he be of soul who could pass by
A sight so touching in its majesty:

This City now doth like a garment wear
The beauty of the morning: silent, bare,
Ships, towers, domes, theatres, and temples lie

Open unto the fields, and to the sky;
All bright and glittering in the smokeless air.
Never did sun more beautifully steep
In his first splendour valley, rock, or hill;
Ne'er saw I, never felt, a calm so deep!
The river glideth at his own sweet will:
Dear God! the very houses seem asleep;
And all that mighty heart is lying still!'

William Wordsworth
'September 1802
Composed upon Westminster Bridge'

CONTENTS

FOREWORD

by Alderman Michael Bear, Lord Mayor of the City of London, 2010-11
Master, The Guildhall Lodge No 3116, 2011-12

THE RIGHT HONOURABLE THE LORD MAYOR
ALDERMAN MICHAEL BEAR

THE MANSION HOUSE, LONDON EC4N 8BH
TELEPHONE 020-7626 2500
FACSIMILE 020-7623 9524

Dear Reader,

It is a pleasure for me to preface the new edition of this small volume on a different historic aspect of our Square Mile by my fellow freeman and City of London guide, Yasha Beresiner. Our City is interspersed with innumerable stunning buildings, ancient locations and extraordinary sites and this guide will allow you to enjoy and identify the many wonders that surround us all.

The singular geographic positioning and strategic location of our walled City were identified early in the 11th Century and those very special privileges granted to the citizens of London alone, by William I in 1067 are still enjoyed to this very day. A very long history brought to light and emphasised in the pages of this little book.

I hope you enjoy reading it and that you enjoy our historic and very special City.

Alderman Michael Bear
Lord Mayor

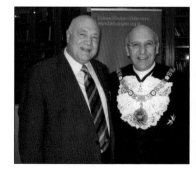

Alderman Bro Michael Bear, Lord Mayor, with the author, Bishopgate, June 2011.

BIBLIOGRAPHY & CREDITS

Ars Quatuor Coronatorum (AQC) Transactions of the Quatuor Coronati Lodge 2076. Volumes 1886-2004. Various articles, notes and comments.

Bradley, Simon and Pevsner, Nikolaus: *London 1: The City of London* Penguin Books, London, 1999

Cappin, J. M.: *London Coffee House Lodges* Lodge of Research Transactions (Leicester), Vol 109, 2000

Hart, John: long-standing friend and colleague, proof reader and teacher

Megarry, Mr Justice: *Inns Ancient and Modern* The Sheldan Lecture, 1971

Peabody, David: fellow member of QC lodge, researcher and source for the majority of the illustrations

Smyth, Frederick: *Freemasonry in Fiction* AQC 93, 1980

Taylor, Paul: guide *par excellence* and dedicated mentor to so many of us

Unwin, George: *The Gilds and Companies of London* London, 1963

Weinreb, Ben and Hibbert, Christopher: *The London Encyclopaedia* London, 1992

Zanelli, Leo: excellent photographer, advisor and counsellor and a great friend

ABOUT THE AUTHOR

Yasha Beresiner was born in Turkey in 1940, had his primary education in England and is a Faculty of Law graduate of the Hebrew University of Jerusalem. He settled in London in 1969. In 2001–02 he served as Master of the Worshipful Company of Makers of Playing Cards, one of the City's ancient Livery Guilds. He is a City of London Guide and the Editor of the Guide's Association Magazine. He has been an active Freemason in England, Italy and Israel since 1975 and is a Past Master of the Quatuor Coronati Lodge, the Premier Lodge of Masonic Research. In 1980 he converted his hobbies to a full time business and is currently trading in collectables through his website *www.intercol.co.uk*

By the same author:

The Paper Tiger — Stayman, 1968 (Arab-Israeli 1967 War)

Catalogue of Colombian Currency — Stanley Gibbons, 1972

The Story of Paper Money — David & Charles, 1976

Collectors' Guide to Paper Money — Andre Deutsch/Stein, 1979

British County Maps — A Guide — ACC Woodbridge, 1985 (British Library Award)

The O-P Catalogue of Playing Cards — InterCol, London, 1995

Masonic Curiosities and more... — ANZMRC Victoria, Australia, 2000

Royal Arch: 4th degree of the Antients — Batham lecture —Supreme Grand Chapter of England, 2000

Masonically Speaking — Lewis Masonic, 2007

The Freemason's Handbook of Toasts, Speeches and Responses — Lewis Masonic, 2009

INTRODUCTION

In November 2001 I was honoured to be elected the Master of The Worshipful Company of Makers of Playing Cards, one of the City of London's ancient Livery Companies, which was granted its charter by Charles II in 1628. I felt at the time duty bound to improve my knowledge of the City beyond the courses offered by the Corporation of London (now named the City of London Corporation) for the benefit of liverymen and others. What better way than by enrolling in the Guide's Course, which already had an excellent reputation? It was a wise decision. Before we were halfway through the course, inspired by the late and much-lamented Katrine Prince and the indefatigable Paul Taylor, I was, just like all of my colleagues, hooked on the 'Square Mile'. Following the presentation of our certificates by the then Lord Mayor, Sir Michael Oliver, at the Mansion House in June of the following year, I immediately invited family first and friends thereafter, week after week, on the City walks which had so enthralled me during the course. It does not take long, however, to run out of family members and even friends can become evermore reluctant to go on yet another walk. The alternative to walking alone or losing the fascinating knowledge that I had only just begun to acquire was to join 'The Streets of London', a quasi-professional body of some 15 qualified guides. We each prepare our own specialised walks for publication in a bi-annual leaflet. My interest in the history of Freemasonry, which I had developed over the past two decades or so, now served me well. Freemasonry and the City of London sat comfortably side by side and this booklet is the result of those two combined interests.

The booklet is intended both as a do-it-yourself guide to the walk and as a general historical survey of some City sites and of related aspects of Masonic interest. I have selected 26 locations between Freemasons' Hall (incidentally just outside the boundaries of the City — yet a logical and convenient starting point) and The Royal Exchange in the Bank. The direct route is a mere 20-minute brisk walk. With this guidebook in your hand and following the route indicated, the walk will take you two hours or so through 2,000 years of history.

The booklet covers just one of many possible walks combining City sites of historical interest with elements of Freemasonry in its various manifestations. Sometimes there is a direct link and relevance — when, for example, you walk down the quaint Mason's Avenue. At other times the Masonic connection is tenuous or non-existent. In this latter case let us remember, whilst avoiding any discourse as to the origins of Freemasonry, that a *speculative* Freemason uses and applies to modern charitable practices the emblems and symbols of the ancient operative working Masons' trade. In this context alone every building, every church and mansion that surrounds us as we walk in the City will be a constant reminder of our Masonic heritage and ancestry.

Enjoy your walk!

The skyline of London has changed much over the years but walking its streets is a constant reminder of our heritage. With kind permission of the Guildhall Library, City of London

PART I: THE CITY OF LONDON

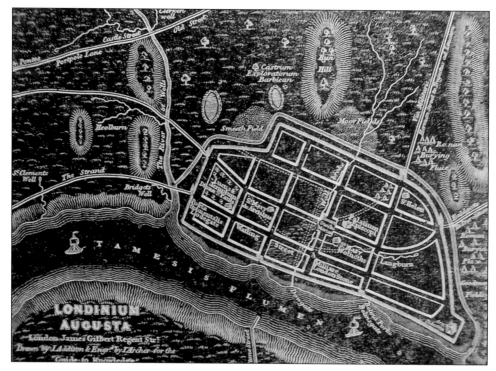

The City of London — An Historical Survey

When the word 'City' is used the emphasis is on the single square mile that distinguishes the City of London from every other city in the world. 'The Square Mile' (a term that is loosely used and incorporates the city and its liberties) is easily identifiable by the boundaries set by the Romans in the year AD200 when they built a defensive wall, parts of which are extant today, and on which our medieval predecessors added their own extensions.

These were the boundaries so well identified by William I in 1066 as encircling wealth and potentially lucrative for the Crown. They formed the basis of those very special arrangements he came to with the citizens of the City. Londoners alone would be directly responsible to the Monarch, by-passing Parliament and electing their own

The City boundaries set by the Romans in the year AD200. Guildhall

Mayor and officers with control over their territory within the delineated boundaries, independent of the rule of centralised Government. This arrangement holds true today.

The Thames

Following Julius Caesar's unsuccessful attempt to invade England in 55BC, Roman legions landed in Kent in AD43 and began their drive towards the northwest in the direction of Colchester. Their path suddenly came to a standstill by the River Thames. They selected the most favourable point to ford the river and later built a bridge. It was to become the first London Bridge, just a few yards from the site of the current bridge, and

'Old Father Thames' is 215 miles (346 kilometres) in length, from an 18th-century print. YB

Londinium, the new trading settlement in the Empire, was born. It did not take long for the fast-growing city to become an important centre for goods and general trading. The River Thames was, of course, there long before the Romans arrived. Its name is from the early Celtic word for 'a wide or broad river'. Whilst the Thames flows past a huge number of famous buildings, including the Houses of Parliament, Westminster Abbey and Somerset House, it is only the section from The Temple to The Tower of London, on the boundary of the City, that defines the southern border of the City itself. The City boundary is drawn through the centre of the river and extends to the southern extremes of London, Southwark and Blackfriars Bridges.

'Old Father Thames' is 215 miles (346 kilometres) in length, with its source in the Cotswolds. As it flows past London Bridge the Thames widens on its approach to the famous and historic naval town of Greenwich. Today the river is cleaner and better maintained than at any time in its history. The best evidence is the huge variety of wildlife now in its waters and on its banks.

Queen Boudicca

The Romans will have been surprised by the strength and support for the formidable Queen Boudicca and the rebellion she led in AD60. The Iceni tribe originated in modern-day East Anglia and targeted Londinium and its 30,000 settlers, both Romans and indigenous farmers and merchants. The trading centre was soon razed to the ground. Eighty thousand Romans and Britons were killed in the ensuing bloody days and Boudicca survived the final battle to return home and poison herself. The City was quickly rebuilt. A military fort stood at the northwest corner and a basilica and forum, the largest in Western Europe, were completed in AD150. Today Gracechurch Street bisects the site almost to perfection.

Roman London

A governor's palace was probably built in modern Cannon Street, facing the Thames. Remnants of the Temple of Mithras were found near Walbrook during construction work in the 1950s and are laid out at the Temple Court in Queen Victoria Street.

In December 2002 a construction crew uncovered the remains of an 1,800-year-old Roman bathhouse with a series of stone and tiled rooms intact, one housing a hot bath and another a cold plunge pool. Many of these artefacts are displayed in the Museum of London. Meanwhile London was growing in stature and commercial importance. Around the year AD200 the Romans extended the ramparts of the military fort to build a defensive wall surrounding the whole City. The boundary thus formed has more or less dictated the shape and size of the City ever since. At its peak, preceding the decline of the Roman Empire at the start of the 5th century, the population of the City reached forty-five thousand inhabitants. When the Romans abandoned London circa AD400, the defenceless City ceased its trading

Remnants of the Temple of Mithras were found in the 1950s. LZ

activities and became desolate and neglected and around AD500 it entered a period that has become known as 'The Dark Ages'.

Saxons

The Saxons, when they first arrived in the early 6th century from Angeln, now in Lower Saxony, established themselves west of the City, outside the walled boundaries in what is now the Strand and Charing Cross. Their settlement became known as *Lundenwic*. In 604 a Bishop of London was appointed for a short period at the time of the building of the first St Paul's Cathedral on the very site of the present one. The geographical location of the City, however, with the Thames on one side and protected and defined by the wall, was too strategic to be ignored. By the middle of the 7th century the City was once more growing and expanding. As London began to prosper over the next two centuries it also began to attract the attention of the aggressive Danish Vikings who periodically sailed up the Thames and attacked it.

The Danes

Events reached a peak in 851 when the Danes arrived at the very heart of the City with three hundred and fifty longboats and burned London to the ground. In 878 King Alfred the Great established a Kingdom of all England. Within a decade he had re-established London, now named *Lundenburg*, within the old Roman city walls. Following his death, however, the Danes resumed their attacks — soon occupying the City. One event, the futile attempt of the Saxons to fend the Vikings off London Bridge, has been immortalised in the nursery rhyme 'London Bridge is Falling Down'.

In 1017 the Danish king Canute came to power and united the Danes with the Anglo-Saxons, once more allowing the City to prosper. When Canute died, the Anglo-Saxons again took control under Edward The Confessor who, as a Norman sympathiser, began the strong French influence England was to experience over the next three centuries. Edward reinstated the Abbey at Westminster and moved his whole Court to London, making it the seat of the royal residence. Although London was not the capital of England (Winchester enjoyed that privilege), it was now the largest and most prosperous city in Britain.

Medieval London

The medieval history of London begins on Christmas Day 1066, when William I was crowned King of England in Westminster Abbey. Though commonly referred to as 'William the Conqueror', this did not apply to the citizens of London with whom, as stated above, he had a special relationship.

William built his fortified White Tower, now part of the complex known as The Tower of London, in the southeast corner outside the City wall, to keep a watch on the citizens whilst at a safe distance. At first the Tower acted as a royal abode. It housed the Royal Mint and the Treasury, and saw the beginnings of a zoo. It was much later, in the 16th century, that it became famous as a

The complex of buildings known as the Tower of London. LZ

prison. In 1097 William II began to build the new Palace of Westminster, which was to become the prime royal residence throughout the Middle Ages. Thus the royal household and Parliament were at the two extremes outside the City boundaries, which allowed the merchant citizens to concentrate and prosper as a commercial and trading entity.

City Rights

As a prosperous and independent body the City's influence was substantial. On William II's death in 1100 his brother Henry sought the support of Londoners to maintain his grip on the throne and rewarded them by enhancing the rights and privileges granted to the City by his father in 1067. Londoners now had the right to levy taxes and, more importantly, to elect their own Sheriff. The population of London at this time was about 18,000, compared to the 45,000 inhabitants estimated at the height of the Roman presence in the City.

Richard I (reigned 1189–99) acknowledged the right of London to self-government, and the election of the first Mayor, Henry Fitz-Ailwyn, took place in 1189. This right was confirmed by later monarchs and was embedded in the Magna Carta in June 1215, in clause 13, which reads: 'And the city of London shall have all its ancient liberties and free customs, as well by land as by water . . .' It made any attempt to change London's special status all but impossible.

London Bridge

It was during this period of the 13th century that London's first stone bridge was built. The Romans in AD52 had erected the first bridge, built of timber. It was vulnerable to fire and flood, as were the subsequent ones. It was not until 1187 that William Rufus put Peter de Colechurch (d.1205) in charge of building a lasting bridge of stone. It took 30 years to complete the new Colechurch bridge. Over the years, the width of the piers was extended, causing increased restriction to the flow of water under the bridge. Many lost their lives trying to negotiate the bridge rapids. Meanwhile the number of buildings on the bridge continued to increase and the silhouette changed constantly. The early houses on the bridge were made with timber frames and supported by beams, which allowed them to overhang the bridge. Raised galleries from the top storey of each house linked it to the one on the opposite side. The shops were gaily painted, with counters projecting into the centre of the bridge street. Ironically the buildings were saved from the Great Fire of 1666 because of an earlier fire in 1639, which destroyed one third of the houses on the City bank of the bridge. Following an Act of Parliament in 1756 all of the bridge's buildings were cleared, together with the outer gates and fortifications.

It was more than 600 years before another bridge was built on the same site. On 15

The first Mayor, Henry Fitz-Ailwyn, 1189. Guildhall

A View of London-Bridge *after the late* Fire, *taken (and drawn by* W.ͬ *Boitaͬ*

In 1825 work started on a new London Bridge, on the same site as the medieval bridge it replaced. The medieval bridge, complete with buildings, is shown in this 18th-century print. Guildhall

13

June 1825 the foundation stone for the new London Bridge, designed by Sir John Rennie (1794-1874), was laid. William IV and Queen Adelaide formally opened it in August 1831. This was the London Bridge that the American McCulloch Oil Corporation purchased in 1968. A year earlier the London Bridge Act empowered the Corporation to build a new bridge and the one by Sir John Rennie was dismantled and replaced section-by-section with a new concrete structure. Rennie's original stones were transported in parts and completely re-assembled at Lake Havasu City in the USA, where 'Old London Bridge' remains a popular tourist site with transport across the bridge available on red double-decker buses. Rumours persist that the Americans in purchasing London Bridge presumed the term to be generic and thought that they were purchasing the more extravagant Tower Bridge. They are, nonetheless, happy with their acquisition. Queen Elizabeth II officially opened our own present London Bridge, the third stone structure, in 1973.

City Events

The potted history of the City is marked by many events relevant to 'The Square Mile' in particular. In 1381 the followers of Wat Tyler in the well-documented 'Peasants' Revolt' invaded the City. The cause of the revolt was not centred on the City but aimed at the advisors of Richard II. Nonetheless the peasants did not resist the temptation offered by their occupation of London, and houses and shops were freely looted. Famously, the Lord Mayor, William Walworth (d.1385), stabbed Wat Tyler to death in a confrontation at Smithfield. When Edward IV made his move to gain the throne in 1461, the citizens of London supported him. In gratitude the newly elected king knighted many of the city merchants. History was also made in 1477 when, on his return from Bruges, William Caxton (?1422–1491) printed the first book in England on his new printing press at the sign of the Red Pale in Westminster. On his death his apprentice Wynkyn de Worde moved to St Bride's courtyard in Fleet Street and established the very long-standing association of that area with the printing trade and the press in particular.

The Streets of London

The City today has hundreds of alleyways and lanes reminiscent of the maze of twisting streets of medieval times. The half-timbered, whitewashed houses with straw roofing were under constant threat of fire, which frequently erupted, notwithstanding legislation passed to ensure householders had fire-fighting equipment on hand. As early as the 13th century a law was passed requiring new houses to use slate for roofing but the ordinance was ignored, to the detriment of the house owners. Most of the streets in the City were named after the particular trade practised on them. The names are extant today: Threadneedle Street was the tailor's district, at Fish Street a weekly market day was held, on Milk Street cows were kept for milking and the bakeries were situated on Bread Street.

City Administration

The government of the City was by the Mayor — subsequently to be known as the Lord Mayor — and the Common Council elected from the ranks of the merchant guilds, the City Livery Companies. Amongst them, relevant to us, was also The Company of Masons whose first regulations were promulgated in 1356. These guilds effectively ran the City and controlled commerce. The representatives of the various guilds met regularly at the Guildhall. The annual election of Sheriffs in June by Liverymen in Common Hall and the subsequent election of the Lord Mayor today traces its origins to this early 15th century practice. When Henry VII took the throne in 1485, the population of the City of London was about 75,000. By 1600 that figure had risen to 200,000.

The City of London's alleyways and lanes are reminiscent of medieval times. LZ

Tudors

London under the Tudors was a prosperous, bustling city. Henry VIII's dissolution of the 13 religious houses in London had a strong effect on the City with several of the monasteries within its boundaries converted for private use or pulled down for building materials. The street names throughout the City are all that remain of the one-time extensive monastic lands: the Minories, the convent of the Order of St. Clare, founded in 1293 by Edmund, Earl of Lancaster, brother to Edward I; Blackfriars, the Catholic Order of Preachers (*Ordo Praedicatorum*), more commonly known as the Dominican Order, founded by Saint Dominic in the early 13th century; and Whitefriars, the Carmelites. John Stowe's *Survey of London* published in 1598 gives us a unique and wonderful if somewhat pedantic survey of the City before the fire of 1666. Stowe was a tailor who dedicated the last years of his life to a detailed study of every aspect of life in the City. Much of what we know today of Tudor London and its history is thanks to his annotations. John Stowe was buried at the Church of St Andrew Undershaft in Leadenhall in 1605, where a marble monument to his memory is the focal point of a quaint ceremony. On 5 April every three years (on his birthday) the Lord Mayor or his representative places a new quill pen in Stowe's hand. The old quill, with a copy of *Stowe's Survey*, is presented to the child who wrote the best essay on London during the year.

Health and Sanitation

The early 17th century saw, to the great relief of Londoners, the completion of the New River Head at Finsbury. Until then, almost unbelievably, the water scheme incorporated both the sewage and drinking water into one system. Only the rich had their own private water wells and others may have been able to afford to purchase their drinking water from water-carriers.

For the majority, however, the health hazard was horrendous. In 1608 an Act of Parliament granted the Corporation the right to channel the water from Hertfordshire to Chadwell. It was a massive engineering project, collecting clean water from 40 miles away and bringing it to the large cisterns at Finsbury and then a final delivery to the City in pipes made of hollowed elm trunks.

Sir John Swynnerton, Lord Mayor in 1612, opened the New River Company on 29 September 1613. The scheme was improved upon in later years, allowing everyone access to purified water, and London's health status changed dramatically.

Oliver Cromwell, Lord Protector of the Commonwealth. LZ

16

London Politics

As the dark clouds of the English Civil War gathered, Charles I was unable to gain the support of Londoners. The City helped finance the Parliamentary efforts against the King who was eventually beheaded in Whitehall on 30 January 1649. At this time we also come across the earliest evidence of Freemasonry in England: Elias Ashmole records in his well-publicised diary his initiation into Freemasonry on 16 October 1646.

The Protectorate and Commonwealth under Oliver Cromwell followed Charles' death but the restoration of the Monarchy brought Charles II to the throne within eleven short years, in 1660. The historical period that follows under the Stuart monarchy is dominated by two disasters: the Great Plague and the devastating Great Fire.

The Plague

In the long, dry summer of 1665 London, well beyond the City boundaries, once again found itself in the grip of a plague.

There had been no fewer then 16 plagues in the City since 1348 but this time it was different, more virulent and destructive than ever before. It was brought over by immigrants from Holland and quickly caused panic among the citizens who were witnessing victims die within hours of catching the virus. Families who were suspected of suffering the illness were barricaded in their homes, left there to die of starvation and in misery. The Lord Mayor in 1664, Sir John Lawrence, under the erroneous assumption that cats and dogs carried the disease, ordered them killed, thus eliminating the natural enemies of the rats, which were the true carriers of the disease. Those who could, fled the City, including members of the Court of Common Council, doctors and priests and those with the financial means to do so. During the three months that the plague raged through the City some 100,000 lives were lost.

There had been 16 plagues in the City since 1348. Guildhall

The Fire

Londoners had not had time to catch their breath before a second calamity, this time contained within the boundaries of the City, descended upon them. On the night of 2 September 1666 a small fire in a bakery in Pudding Lane was spotted but ignored as being of no consequence. The Lord Mayor of the City in 1665, Sir Thomas Bludworth, woken in the middle of the night to be warned of it, had a quick look and famously uttered the well-recorded comment that 'a woman could piss it out'. By morning, fanned by a persistent easterly wind, the fire had spread uncontrollably through the City's narrow lanes and close-packed streets.

The fire's spread was facilitated by the wooden houses whose inhabitants had moved to the riverfront, waiting for the fire to subside. It didn't. It raged for four days

The fire spread uncontrollably through the City. Guildhall

destroying everything in its path. Ironically the City authorities, the Lord Mayor and Court of Common Council, could have done more to arrest the fire on the first day had they not feared breaching the citizens' property rights. The co-ordinated destruction of one row of the wooden houses in the path of the fire would have put a stop to its spreading from lane to lane. Instead the Mayor's fears made him act indecisively, to the fatal detriment of the City. The fire finally came to an end in the Temple area, the ancient medieval church and the surrounding stone buildings south of Smithfield. In Giltspur Street, at the first floor level is the 'Golden Boy' statue, to mark the point where the Great Fire finally stopped. Because the fire spread 'from Pudding Lane to Pie Corner', Londoners felt that they had been punished for greed.

The Golden Boy hugs his belly, symbolising the sin of gluttony. The statistical toll of the fire makes horrendous reading. Although it is thought that only eight lives were lost, no less than four-fifths of the city was completely destroyed. A total of 13,000 buildings, 52 City Livery Halls and 89 churches, including old St Paul's Cathedral, were reduced to ashes. On 5 February 1667, instigated by Charles II, the Building Regulation Act was passed by Parliament 'for the better regulation, uniformity, and gracefulness of architecture'. It changed the face of the City, replacing the plaster and timber houses with ones of slab and stone which are in evidence to this day.

Sir Christopher Wren

The City had to be rebuilt and Sir Christopher Wren, friend of Charles II, was invited to present his vision of a new City. Wren did so within weeks. Broad

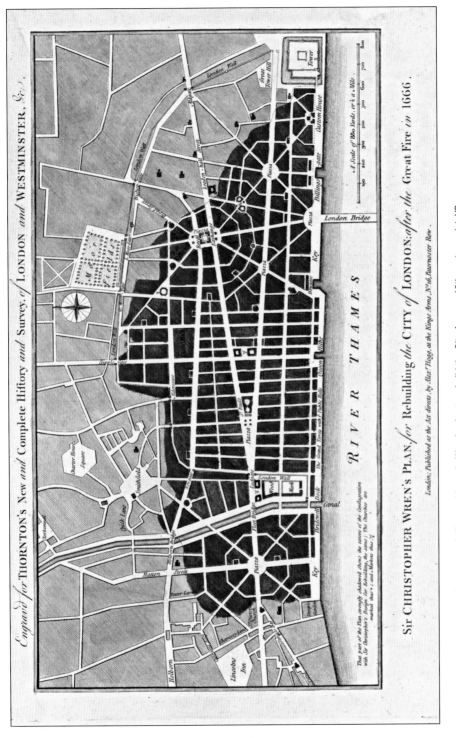

Engrav'd for THORNTON's New and Complete History and Survey, of LONDON and WESTMINSTER, &c.

Sir CHRISTOPHER WREN's PLAN, for Rebuilding the CITY of LONDON: after the Great Fire in 1666.

London: Published as the Act directs, by Alex.r Hogg, at the Kings Arms, N.o 16, Paternoster Row.

A Scale of 880 Yards, or ½ a Mile.

That part of the Plan strongly shadowed shews the extent of the Conflagration with Sir Christopher's Design for Rebuilding, the same: The Churches are marked thus ✚; and Markets thus ▨

RIVER THAMES

A fanciful grid pattern replaced the warren of alleys and lanes in Wren's plan to rebuild the City, from an 18th-century print. YB

19

boulevards and straight streets with wide-open piazzas radiated out from a central square in front of London Bridge, now the Monument. The fanciful grid pattern, intended to replace the warren of alleys, lanes and streets, was a costly proposal. This was not the reason, however, that it was rejected. Following the fire, land disputes erupted and the sixteen newly appointed 'Fire Judges' (immortalised in the paintings commissioned from John Michael Wright in 1670 to 1675 by the Court of Aldermen) had their hands full. The only way to resolve the many claims brought before them was to rebuild the houses and streets as close to their original pre-fire standing as possible. The result is that today the City landscape, the street layout, is effectively indistinguishable from that of the medieval town. Wren, meanwhile, with the King's assistance, persuaded the Church Commissioners to give him some leeway in rebuilding St Paul's Cathedral and the churches surrounding it.

His astounding handiwork is in evidence throughout the City today.

Riots

The 1780 Gordon Riots, named after their vociferous leader Lord George Gordon (1751–1793), were instigated by the 1778 Relief Act, which repealed harsh legislation dating back to the 17th century and granted basic rights to Catholics. The anti-Catholic riots that followed began with a march through the City to Parliament to present a petition requesting the repeal of the Relief Act and demanding a return to Catholic repression. The violence continued for 10 days, with running battles between the authorities and demonstrators who were attacking Catholics in the street. By the time the riot was under control, twelve thousand troops had been deployed and over seven hundred people had been killed. George Gordon was acquitted of high treason but the Lord Mayor of London in 1779, Brackley Kennett, was fined £1,000 for negligence of his duties.

Victorian London

By the time we reach the Victorian period in the 19th century, the City formed only a small part of Metropolitan London. Nonetheless it remained a prosperous, independent and influential sector. The buildings and affluent development within the Square Mile at this time were in stark contrast to some parts of London where overcrowded slums were inhabited by people in the worst conditions imaginable. The overall population during the century surged from less than one million in 1800 to well over six million at the end of Queen Victoria's reign in January 1901. The City, although less affected by the plight of the rest of a London seemingly unable to provide the basic needs for its citizens, contributed generously towards improvement and recovery. A major project was to rid London of the foul-smelling heavy air caused by a combination of coal-fired stoves and pitiful sanitation. Raw sewage was still being dumped into the Thames in large quantities and the health hazard continued. Finally, matters were brought to a welcome end by Joseph Bazalgette (1819–1891). In 1856 London's Metropolitan Board of Works was established and it elected Bazalgette as its first, and only, chief engineer. This unsung hero was almost solely responsible for the building of over 1,300 miles (2,100 kilometres) of tunnels and pipes, diverting the sewage out of London. The practical result of Bazalgette's work was a dramatic drop in the death rate, which had been caused by outbreaks of cholera. Joseph Bazalgette has rightly been credited with being as influential in improving the appearance of London as Sir Christopher Wren.

The Railway

Early in the 19th century the City was involved, from its start, in the golden age of the steam railway. The first station was built at London Bridge in 1836 followed by major stations at Euston and Paddington and, in 1841, Fenchurch Street in the heart of the

THE CITY TERMINUS OF THE SOUTH-EASTERN RAILWAY, CANNON-STREET.—SEE PAGE 170.

THE MOSQUE OF GHOLAUM MAHOMED, CALCUTTA. ... GOLD-MINING WORKS IN NEW ZEALAND.

The golden age of the steam railway — an Illustrated London News picture of Cannon Street station, 1866. DP

City. The first underground railway from Paddington to Farringdon Road was completed in 1863. Of Masonic relevance at this time is the election and installation of the Prince of Wales, later King Edward VII, as Grand Master of the United Grand Lodge of England. He was publicly known as a Freemason and a great promoter of the Craft. He brought the fraternity into fashion and membership of the society swelled accordingly. Meanwhile, the growth in population, which had appeared to be reaching a peak in the late Victorian period, continued into the 20th century.

City at War

The City suffered badly during both World Wars. On 31 May 1915 the first Zeppelin bombs fell near the Guildhall, killing 39 people. All told, enemy bombings of the City resulted in 650 deaths. The end of the

During the Second World War, thousands of children were transported — 'evacuated' — out of London. LZ

The controversial Barbican complex. LZ

war in 1918 saw another surge in London's population, which neared seven and a half million inhabitants in 1921. As Hitler's threats began to have an impact in the years leading up to the Second World War, large numbers of children moved out of London to the surrounding countryside.

A monument has been recently placed outside Liverpool Street station, to where many of the children from Europe arrived, to commemorate the event. The City was to suffer severely from the German 'Blitz' that followed. Over one third of the City was to be destroyed by German bombs dropped from aircraft using the Thames and St Paul's Cathedral as markers to direct their path over the City. Seventeen of Sir Christopher Wren's churches were damaged, some never restored to their former glory. Sixteen acres in the southwest of the City were totally flattened and numerous historic buildings destroyed. Fatalities were heavy. The death toll stood at 32,000 with over 50,000 injured. Recovery of the City, and London as a whole, was rapid and complete. The Barbican complex, if somewhat controversial, is today the pride of the City, totally elevated above street level with the Museum of London as its centrepiece.

The financial institutions were soon back in action and the City regained its international standing.

Today the many varied and fascinating facets of the City of London, commercial, geographic, demographic and, not least, historical, make 'The Square Mile' the envy of the world's capitals.

PART II: THE WALK

STOP 1. Freemasons' Hall

DIRECTIONS: The address of Freemasons' Hall is Great Queen Street, London WC2 and the switchboard telephone number is 020 7831 9811. Access is easy by Underground to Holborn Station on the Central and Piccadilly Lines. Exit into Kingsway and turn left. The second street on your right, at the traffic lights where you can cross over safely, is Great Queen Street. The entrance to Freemasons' Hall is on the left past the Connaught Rooms.

Of Masonic Interest: **Freemasons' Hall**

Freemasons' Hall is the home of the United Grand Lodge of England and some three hundred thousand Freemasons in England and Wales. It is situated in Great Queen Street running between Covent Garden and Kingsway, an extension of Long Acre. It is an imposing building in the art deco style, situated in the very heart of the capital on the edge of Covent Garden. It is a short walking distance from the famous Temple Church, the seat of the original Knights Templar, now even more immortalised by Dan Brown's *The Da Vinci Code*.

The First Hall

This building occupies two and a quarter acres along much of Great Queen Street. It was completed in 1933 and is dedicated to the memory of the 3,225 British Freemasons who died on active service in the First World War. It was known as The Masonic Peace Memorial and reverted to the name Freemasons' Hall at the outbreak of war in 1939. It is the third hall built on the same site. The first Freemasons' Hall consisted of two adjoining houses purchased in 1775 by the Premier Grand Lodge. Thomas Sandby (1721–1798), the architect, engineer and draughtsman, was appointed to amalgamate the houses with a Grand Hall between them. The resulting building had The Freemasons' Tavern as a frontage.

Bro Soane

Considerable changes took place after the Union of the two Grand Lodges in 1813 when the Duke of Sussex invited his friend, the famous architect of the Bank of England, Sir John Soane (1753–1837) to add extensions to the building. Having submitted his proposals as a layman, John Soane was soon initiated, passed and raised as a Freemason on the same day and given high rank to add a Masonic dimension to the respect he very much enjoyed as an architect. When Frederick Cockerell (1833–1878) built the second Masons' Hall in the 1860s he incorporated Sandby's original Grand Hall of 1775 into his building and sadly much of John Soane's later work was replaced. Parts of the building were destroyed in the fire of 1883.

New Hall

In 1908 the building was divided, separating the dining area, and it was finally demolished to allow the building of the present Hall, which began in 1927. The banqueting suite, where many Masonic dinners are now held, was named The Connaught Rooms after Prince Arthur, Duke of Connaught and Strathearn, Grand Master from 1901 to 1939, and comprises the surviving eastern section of Cockerell's original building. In 1925 the London partnership of H. V. Ashley and Winton Newman won the international architectural competition chaired by Sir Edwin Lutyens. The present Hall is the result and enjoys a very special status: it is the only Grade II listed art deco building in London, preserved 'as built' and in continuous use for its original purpose. It is an impressive edifice by any standards.

Grand Temple

The Grand Temple inside, totally isolated from the adjoining structures, dominates the building. It stands 120 feet in length, 90 feet in width and 62 feet in height. The extraordinary Masonic bronze doors, each weighing one and a quarter tonnes, open onto the impressive chamber that seats 1,700 brethren. The ceiling consists entirely of a mosaic design depicting Masonic emblems and symbols. In addition to the Grand Temple there are 19 other Craft lodge rooms and Royal Arch Temples in the building, as well as offices, meeting rooms and the usual facilities. In recent years the Grand Temple has been hired out for opera performances and musical concerts. The recent performance of Mozart's *Magic Flute* could not have been staged in a more ideal setting.

Museum Notes:
Library & Museum and *Letchworth's*

Grand Lodge houses the well-known Library and Museum situated on the first floor. It is open free of charge to the general public. It is considered to be the largest Masonic library extant and has artefacts and Masonic memorabilia famous worldwide. Free guided tours of the building start at the Library and Museum every weekday from 11.00am hourly until 4.00pm. Call 020 7395 9257 for more information and group bookings. The ground floor now boasts *Letchworth's*, a shop well stocked with Masonic items and books situated within Freemasons' Hall. It was named after Sir Edward Letchworth who was the Grand Secretary of the United Grand Lodge of England from 1892 to 1917.

STOP 2. Great Queen Street

DIRECTIONS: Walk out of the doors of Freemasons' Hall into Great Queen Street and turn right towards Kingsway, Holborn. **STOP (2)** at the end of Great Queen Street at its intersection with Kingsway.

Historical Notes: **Great Queen Street**

The street you walked along is depicted on the Agas map of London dated 1560. The map shows it as a track cutting across Aldwych. By 1612 it had become the first regular street in London noted for the many brick houses. It was first named Queen's Street in honour of Queen Anne of Denmark (1574–1619), who was consort to King James I. Historians are still arguing as to why the street should have been built in the first place. Both the east and west ends of the street initially ran into fields, although the thoroughfare soon developed into a sophisticated residential area. By 1658 it was fully built up, with some distinguished residents. The area where you stand, south of the old Holbourne or Old Bourne, meaning a stream, was the first of the estates purchased by the Knights Templar in 1128, before they moved to the Temple in 1162. In the 17th century this area was considered the wealthy district of London.

STOP 3. The Old Curiosity Shop

DIRECTIONS: At the top of Great Queen Street cross Kingsway to the opposite side and turn right, walking south towards the Aldwych. At Sardinia Street turn left and the first turning to your right is Portsmouth Street. A few yards along on your left **STOP (3)** at one of the oldest buildings extant in London: The Old Curiosity Shop.

Historical Notes: **The Old Curiosity Shop**

This original 1567 building, with an overhanging upper storey, is made up of three floors: a workshop, gallery and shop floor. Until recently the house, which occupies numbers 13 and 14 Portsmouth Street, was exactly what the name suggests: a shop selling curiosities and souvenirs. In 1998 it was taken over by the present tenants who trade in shoes and clothing. It is a listed building. The shop has been immortalised in Charles Dickens' fourth novel. The plot follows the life of Little Nell and her grandfather, who are residents of The Old Curiosity Shop.

Of Masonic Interest: **Charles Dickens' Writings**

Charles Dickens (1812–1870) was not a Freemason. He does, however, on several occasions in his novels refer to the Craft. In his first book, *Sketches by Boz* published in 1836, in scene 19 *Public Dinners* there is a humorous description of a banquet of 'The Indigent Orphans' Friends Benevolent Institution', which takes place at The Freemasons' in Great Queen Street.

'Let us suppose you are induced to attend a dinner of this description — "Indigent Orphans' Friends' Benevolent Institution" we think it is . . . and you deposit yourself . . . to the very door of the Freemasons', round which a crowd of people are assembled to witness the entrance of the indigent orphans' friends . . . The first thing that strikes you, on your entrance, is the astonishing importance of the committee . . . the knives and forks look as if they had done duty at every public dinner in London since the accession of George the First . . . You have no time to debate the matter, however, for the waiters (who have been arranged in lines down the room, placing the dishes on table) retire to the lower end; out burst the orchestra, up rise the visitors, in march fourteen stewards, each with a long wand in his hand, like the evil genius in a pantomime; then the chairman, then the titled visitors; they all make their way up the room, as fast as they can, bowing, and smiling, and smirking, and looking remarkably amiable. The applause ceases, grace is said, the clatter of plates and dishes begins; and every one appears highly gratified, either with the presence of the distinguished visitors, or the commencement of the anxiously expected dinner.'

'The Old Curiosity Shop' is one of the oldest buildings extant in London. LZ

The book is illustrated with engravings by George Cruikshank and the relevant etching is reminiscent of a painting by Thomas Stothard, RA (1755–1834) completed some years earlier. It shows Chevalier Ruspini presenting the Freemasons' Charity children to the Trustees and Governors on their Anniversary at Freemasons' Hall. In 1802 the painting was engraved and published as the well-known print by Francesco Bartolozzi.

In *Barnaby Rudge: A Tale of the Riots of 'Eighty*, published in 1841, Dickens introduces the Society of *Prentice Knights* (later the *United Bull-Dogs*) with an easily recognisable satirical description of its ceremonial:

'To this the novice made rejoinder, that he would take the vow, though it should choke him; and it was accordingly administered with many

impressive circumstances, among which the lighting up of the two skulls with a candle-end inside of each, and a great many flourishes with the bone, were chiefly conspicuous. ...
Mr Tappertit, flourishing the bone, knocked nine times therewith upon one of the skulls...
"Prentice" said the mighty captain, "who waits without?" The 'prentice made answer that a stranger was in attendance, who claimed admission into that secret society of 'Prentice Knights, and a free participation in their rights, privileges, and immunities. Thereupon Mr Tappertit flourished the bone again and, giving the other skull a prodigious rap on the nose, exclaimed "Admit him! . ." There soon appeared at the same door, two other 'prentices, having between them a third, whose eyes were bandaged, and who was attired in a bag-wig, and a broad-skirted coat, trimmed with tarnished lace; and who was girded with a sword, in compliance with the laws of the Institution.'

And finally in *Bleak House*, published 1853:

'Volumnia is charmed to hear that her delight is come. He is so original, such a stolid creature, such an immense being for knowing all sorts of things and never telling them! Volumnia is persuaded that he must be a Freemason. Is sure he is at the head of a lodge, and wears short aprons, and is made a perfect idol of with candlesticks and trowels. These lively remarks the fair Dedlock delivers in her youthful manner, while making a purse.'

It is interesting to note that on Saturday 2 November 1867 Dickens himself was honoured with a Public Banquet given for him at Freemasons' Hall in Great Queen Street, which was attended by many dignitaries.

The northern wall of St Clement Danes Church. LZ

STOP 4. Lincoln's Inn

DIRECTIONS: Continue straight down Portsmouth Street and turn right into Portugal Street and immediately left into St Clement's Lane. At the end turn right into Grange Court. On your left is Clement's Inn Gate and steps leading down to the pedestrian path. This will take you out through the gate that leads to the Strand. **STOP (4)** at the end of the path. You will be facing, on the traffic island opposite, the north wall of St Clement Danes Church in the Strand.

Historical Notes: **Inns of Court**

An Inn or *hospitium* meant a town house or mansion. The Lincoln's Inn, which occupies eleven acres of the rectangle formed by High Holborn, Carey Street, the Royal Courts of Justice and Chancery Lane, is one of the four active historic Inns of Court: Lincoln's Inn, Inner Temple, Middle Temple and Gray's Inn, in that order of seniority though not antiquity. Although serving the same functions and duties, the Inns are distinct from each other and practise a friendly

rivalry. Each owns its own private property and enjoys distinctive customs and traditions. The Inns of Court are ancient unincorporated institutions comprised of lawyers who are in absolute control of the legal trade. In 1292 the profession was placed under the control of the judges by Edward I, who brought to an end the activities of the clergy as lawyers. The new professional lawyers now needed a place to meet and congregate and have their own premises where the legal apprentices could be housed. Thus the early Inns of Court were first formed. They are the equivalent to university colleges but for the exclusive use of lawyers. For five centuries and more the Inns of Court have held the power to call to the Bar members who have qualified as Barristers-at-Law. In spite of their antiquity — Lincoln's Inn, for instance, has records that go back to 1422 (Middle Temple 1501, Inner Temple 1505 and Gray's Inn 1569) — these institutions cater for every conceivable aspect of a lawyer's life. The Inns of Court

One of the four active historic Inns of Court: Lincoln's Inn. LZ

are naturally all adjacent to the Courts of Justice towards which we will shortly walk.

Historical Notes: St Clement Danes Church

St Clement Danes Church, not to be confused with St Clement's Church in Eastcheap, lies just outside the boundary of the City of London but has all the characteristics of a City church. It traces its origins to the period of the Danish invasions in the 9th century. Although unaffected by the Great Fire of London in 1666, it was rebuilt by Sir Christopher Wren between 1680 and 1682 and the familiar steeple was added by James Gibbs in 1719. In 1941 the Church was damaged by the German Blitz on London. The restoration was undertaken by Anthony Lloyd in 1955. Three years later St Clement Danes was dedicated to the Royal Air Force and has served that branch of the armed forces ever since.

STOP 5. The Temple Bar Memorial

DIRECTIONS: Walk to your left in front of the Royal Courts of Justice to the second set of pedestrian lights. Cross to the south side and turn to face the street. **STOP (5).**

Straight ahead, on the opposite side of the street, are the impressive white buildings you have just walked past: the Royal Courts of Justice and, rather imposing in the middle of the street to your right, is the Temple Bar Memorial surmounted by an enormous heraldic dragon.

Historical Notes: **The Royal Courts Of Justice**

The imposing white Victorian Gothic buildings that constitute the Royal Courts of Justice are just outside the boundaries of the City of London. They are England's main civil courts and home to both the High Court and the Court of Appeal. The building is huge and occupies a vast area. It was built with 35 million bricks and faced with Portland stone. The wide and daunting entrance hall is intended to be reminiscent of the nave of a Gothic cathedral. The Church architect, George E. Street (1824–1881), wanted the building to have the semblance of a temple to justice. In the interior, which is as magnificent as the façade, there are one thousand rooms connected by three and a half miles of corridors. The centrepiece, so to speak, is the Great Hall with its Italian marble mosaic floor. It extends 230 feet and rises to 80 feet above ground. It has soaring arches and beautiful stained glass windows, which depict the coats of arms of Lord Chancellors and Keepers of the Great Seal. It is considered to be one of the last major Gothic revival buildings in London and, almost surprisingly, was built only in the 1870s and formally opened by Queen Victoria in 1882. The building and the proceedings, which take place in 88 courtrooms, are open to the general public.

The impressive white buildings of the Royal Courts of Justice. LZ

The enormous heraldic dragon which represents the City of London. LZ

Museum Notes: Royal Courts of Justice

The Royal Courts of Justice contain two exhibitions of legal dress, worn by dummies encased in Inca cases. The area on the ground and first floor of the main buildings is open to the public free of charge. The doors are open Monday to Friday from 09:30am to 4:30pm but closed on Public Holidays.

Of Masonic Interest: Masonic Legalities

In February 1997 the Home Affairs Committee of the House of Commons decided to look into the question of Freemasonry in the Police and the Judiciary. The final report was overwhelmingly favourable towards Freemasonry. A long list of judges, magistrates and other members of the judiciary, including Lord Mackay, the Lord Chancellor, and high-ranking policemen, were called as witnesses and:

> 'The Committee conclude that, when the oath (candidates for Masonic initiation take) is read in context, there is nothing in them that would appear sinister, and nothing in the evidence that we have heard that would show a conflict between the oath taken by a judge or policeman and that by a Freemason.
> 'We do not believe that there is anything sinister about Freemasonry, properly observed, and are confident that Freemasonry itself does not encourage malpractice.'

Notwithstanding this positive aspect of the report, the enquiry recommended that a register should be made available to the public of all those involved in the administration of criminal justice and Freemasons should be identified on the register. The United Grand Lodge of England issued a seven point News Release on 25 March 1997 and no further development or action was taken. In May 1997 a new Labour Government came into power and pursued the matter further. A new Home Affairs Committee, under the Chairmanship of Christopher Mullin MP,

was appointed in February 1998. This time there were specific allegations of a Masonic conspiracy involving police corruption. After the initial hearings, the Home Affairs Committee did not pursue the matter further. Yet today, in England, every new member of the judiciary or police has still to sign a form indicating his membership of the Craft, if he is a Freemason, a disconcerting political requirement that has attracted the attention of the Human Rights legislation of the European Courts of Justice.

Historical Notes: Temple Bar Memorial

In the middle of the road, where the Temple Bar once stood, is Sir Horace Jones' monument to Queen Victoria completed in 1872. The large imposing heraldic dragon, the City's logo and symbol, on top of the statue marks this spot as the formal boundary line between Westminster and the City of London. From here you enter 'The Square Mile' and there is a change in the administrative jurisdiction, the police force and rules and regulations by which you now have to behave, with some special privileges if you are a Freeman of the City. The original Roman gate of AD200 was situated some 800 yards to the east at Ludgate Hill. On this spot here, however, where the Strand meets Fleet Street, there is a record going back to 1293 of a 'bar', which was probably no more than a chain or a rod between two wooden posts. The name *Temple Bar* is derived from its vicinity to the Temple area, the 13th century headquarters of the Knights Templar, the area we will soon be entering. The dominant status of the original Temple Bar is emphasised by the numerous state occasions on which it is mentioned throughout history: on 19 September 1356 the Black Prince, Edward Prince of Wales (1330–1376), rode through it accompanied by his prisoner, the King of France, following his victory at the Battle of Poitiers in the Hundred Years War; in 1381, during the Peasants' Revolt, the Temple Bar was badly damaged; and Elizabeth I passed

The old Temple Bar survived the Great Fire of London. LZ

through the gate in 1588 to the tumultuous applause of the citizens celebrating the defeat of the Spanish Armada.

The old Temple Bar survived the Great Fire of London in 1666 but, together with other City Gates, it was neglected and deteriorated to the verge of collapse. It was only by the intervention of King Charles II that, according to some accounts, Sir Christopher Wren was approached in 1670 and commissioned to build the third Temple Bar on the same site. Some scholars believe that it was built by the master masons Thomas Knight and Joshua Marshall. Either way, the imposing gateway, with its wide central archway and pedestrian arches on either side, was built with Portland stone from the quarries in Dorset. It was completed in 1672. Above the central archway was a massive stone structure with niches for statues under a domed summit. These were adorned with four royal statues by the eccentric sculptor John Bushnell (1630–1701) who died insane. On one side are the statues of James I and his consort, Anne of Denmark (of Great Queen Street fame!). On the other side, depicted in Roman costume as was fashionable at the time, are Charles I, who had been executed in 1649, and his elder son, Charles II, restored to the throne in 1660. Not to be forgotten was the inclusion of iron spikes along the top of the gate on which the heads of executed traitors were placed. At the height of the Jacobite Rebellion, in 1745, the site became known as 'Golgotha', translated as 'the place of a skull', owing to the numerous heads displayed on it.

The Temple Bar survived longer than most of the original Roman gates, which had all been demolished by the end of the 18th century. Traffic congestion and expensive maintenance costs finally led the Court of the Common Council in 1877 to remove the Temple Bar and widen Fleet Street to accommodate increasing traffic. This also allowed for the building of the new Royal Courts of Justice. The removal of the Temple

Bar was to be a temporary measure until an alternative City site for the gateway could be established. Thus in January 1878 each stone was numbered and stored in a vacant lot in Farringdon Road. In 1882 Sir Henry Meux, a wealthy London brewer, was induced by Lady Meux, reputedly his banjo-playing barmaid wife, to purchase the lot. In 1889 the Temple Bar was re-erected as a gateway to the Meux property at Theobald's Park, between Enfield in Middlesex and Cheshunt in Hertfordshire. This property was formerly known as Theobald's Palace Estate, and had been the 17th century home of James I and Charles I.

The Corporation of London never lost sight of its original resolution to re-erect the Temple Bar when a suitable site had been located. At the December meeting of the Court of Common Council in 2001 the Corporation agreed to fund the return of the Temple Bar at a cost of £3 million with the support of the Temple Bar Trust and several of the City Livery Companies. The re-erection of the Temple Bar in Paternoster Square, north of St Paul's Cathedral, was completed in November 2004. Later on in the walk we shall have the opportunity to view the original Temple Bar at close quarters.

Of Masonic Interest: **Horace Jones**
Sir Horace Jones (1819–1887) was an active Freemason and among the most notable of English architects of the 19th century. Appointed Architect to the Corporation of the City of London in 1864, he continued in that post until 1887, two years after being knighted for his services.

In addition to the memorial to Queen Victoria, which we have been discussing, Horace Jones' most important work was the famous Tower Bridge, which was completed after his death to amended designs. He is also noted for the colourful and attractive scheme of several London markets run by the City of London Corporation: Smithfield (1866), Billingsgate (1875) and Leadenhall (1881). His many City contributions included the Guildhall Free Library and Museum (1872),

the Guildhall Council Chamber (1884) and the Guildhall School of Music and Drama (completed in 1886). In 1864 Horace Jones was initiated into the Jerusalem Lodge No 197 and became Master in 1869. He gained the high rank — as many architects who became Masons did — of Grand Superintendent of Works from 1882 to 1887, the year of his death. He was buried in West Norwood Cemetery in south London.

Historical Notes:
Heraldic Dragon and The Freedom
The City of London has many ancient emblems and symbols that identify its political independence and sovereignty.

Amongst these are the coat of arms supported by two heraldic dragons with scaly body and wings. They should not be

The City of London's heraldic device of a single dragon. LZ

Horace Jones' most important work was the famous Tower Bridge. Guildhall

confused with the *griffin*, a mythological creature which has the body of a lion and the head of an eagle, generally represented with four legs, wings, a beak and eagle's talons. A shield bearing the heraldic device of a single dragon carrying the City coat of arms marks the City's boundaries. It appears as a statue on some of the main roads leading into the City of London. The same shield will be found on street name plaques and bollards within the City.

Granting of the Freedom of the City of London is probably the oldest ceremony in existence, other than the coronation. The first Freedom was presented in 1237 and indicated that the medieval Freeman in question did not belong to a feudal lord. A Freeman had the right to earn a living and be a landowner. Until 1835 the Freedom of the City and membership in one of the City Livery Companies was prerequisite to being able to exercise a trade within the City of London. The ancient privileges associated with the Freedom are quaint and amusing in a modern context: the right to herd sheep over London Bridge and to go about the City with a drawn sword. A Freeman, if convicted of a capital offence, may be hanged with silken rope. These and many more privileges are listed in the booklet *Rules for the Conduct of Life* every Freeman receives when admitted. They were written in 1737.

No 1 Fleet Street was the site of the Devil Tavern. LZ

STOP 6. The Devil Tavern

DIRECTIONS: Walk a few yards to No 1 Fleet Street, now the home of the famous City bankers Messrs Child & Co. **STOP (6).** On the wall to the left of the main entrance is a blue plaque which reads 'Site of the Devil Tavern demolished 1787'. From here you also have your first glimpse of the length of Fleet Street running eastwards towards St Paul's Cathedral.

Historical Notes: Plaques

The first official London plaques were erected in 1867 by the Royal Society of Arts at the instigation of Liverpool born MP, William Ewart (1798–1869). By 1901 a total of 36 plaques had been erected, the oldest surviving ones commemorating Napoleon III (1808–1873) in King Street, St James's, and the poet John Dryden (1631-1700) in Gerard Street, Soho, both placed *in situ* in 1875. In the City the rectangular glazed plaques mark many historical sites. Similar green plaques are used in Westminster. In total there are some seven hundred official plaques, most of which are blue with white lettering. Since the early 1900s local authorities and private individuals have erected their own plaques in different styles, which can be found in all areas of London.

Of Masonic Interest: The Devil Tavern

The most overt manifestation of Masonic presence in the City of London, and along Fleet Street and in its vicinity in particular, is the one-time preponderance of 17th and 18th century taverns and inns in which Freemasons met.

A tavern was a drinking and eating establishment only, whilst an inn had additional facilities to accommodate an overnight stay in suitable chambers. 'The Devil' would have been as typical of these taverns as any. It was originally named 'The Devil and St Dunstan' because of its proximity to the church. St Dunstan, the Saxon patron saint of goldsmiths, is often depicted carrying pincers in his right hand to recall the medieval legend of the time when he seized the devil by the nose with his red-hot pincers. The Devil Tavern was there before the fire of London of 1666. Pepys mentions it in his diaries on 22 April 1661 when describing King Charles' journey from the Tower to Whitehall:

'. . . and there we had a good room to ourselfs, with wine and good cake, and saw the shew very well — in which it is impossible to relate the glory of that this day... The Bishops came next after the Barons . ... The King, in a most rich imbroidered suit and cloak, looked most nobly. Wadlow, the vintner at the Devil in Fleetstreet, did lead a fine company of souldiers, al young comely men . . .'

The Devil was a large convoluted building with nineteen hearths dispersed in as many rooms. In spite of its location, it was considered to be a City tavern frequented by intellectuals. Samuel Johnson, whose residence we will be visiting later in the walk, moved home to be nearer the tavern. John Evelyn, Wren's contemporary architect and diarist, describes a gathering at The Devil in 1680 attended by one hundred and eighty Members of Parliament. It is not surprising to find that our own Grand Lodge also met here. Although there are no records of the early meetings of the Freemasons following the formation of Grand Lodge in 1717, Anderson's second *Constitutions* of 1738 gives us details of events in the previous years. On page 119 he reports on the meeting held under Grand Master Charles Lennos, Duke of Richmond and Lennox:

'Grand Lodge (met) in due Form at the Devil Temple Bar 20 May 1725 with former Grand Officers and those of 38 Lodges. D G Master Folkes in the Chair prompted a most agreeable Communication.'

Martin Folkes (1690–1754), the English antiquary and President of the Royal Society in 1741, was Deputy Grand Master in 1724. This was two years after the earliest recorded Masonic meeting at The Devil. Lodge number 25 was consecrated at The Devil in

1724 and erased in 1745; the Union Lodge, warranted in 1734, met here and was erased in 1744. So did Lodge 115 in 1729, which moved to Daniel's coffee house in Fleet Street in 1735. These are just a few examples. Grand Lodge returned to The Devil on 24 June 1727. By now proper minutes were being kept and the entry, as an example of several later meetings also held at The Devil, for this date reads:

'[Earl of Inchiquin, G.M.]

At a Quarterly Communication held at the Devil Tavern at Temple Bar on Saturday the 24th of June 1727.

Present.

The Rt Hon the Earl of Inchiquin, Grand Master

Wm Cowper Esq, D G Master

Alexander Chocke Esq, G Warden

Wm Burdon Esq, G Warden

The Minutes of the Last Quarterly Communication were read.

Then the Grand Ma[r]*. Nominated George Payne, Martin ffolkes (sic) and ffrancis (sic) Sorell Esq to be three of the Commee (sic) of Seven for Managing the Bank of Charity pursuant to the Minutes of the 10th of May last . . .'*

In 1640 the Vintner Wadlow purchased The Devil and sold it, twenty-one years later, to Jonathon Barford who, in turn, gave up ownership in 1668 in favour of Richard Taylor. The next ownership recorded is by Messrs Child the bankers who purchased it and rebuilt their bank on the same site in 1788.

STOP 7. The Temple Area

DIRECTIONS: Continue a few yards east along Fleet Street until you reach a stone gateway on your right, headed 'Middle Temple Lane — 1684'. (The gates are closed at night and at weekends.) Enter the Temple area and bear in mind that you are now on private property. Walk down the lane past Brick Court until you are in sight of the impressive Middle Temple Hall on your right.

STOP (7) in the midst of Fountain Court and gardens. This is where, according to Shakespeare, the plucking of the red rose of Lancaster and the white rose of York led to the historic Wars of the Roses (1455–1485).

Historical Notes: **The Middle Temple**
The Gate House through which you walked is the main entrance to the Temple from Fleet Street. In 1520 a second gate was built by Sir Amyas Paulet (1457-1538) and the present one was erected in 1684 by Roger North (1653–1734). The Temple is divided into two sections, Inner and Middle Temples, and is situated in the corridor between the commercial City and the Royal Courts of Justice in Westminster. The Temple, though within the City of London, enjoys special privileges. The Inner Temple — to where we shall be proceeding from here — is identified by its logo, the winged horse Pegasus, whilst the Middle Temple has the Paschal Lamb, the *Agnus Dei,* and the flag of innocence as its symbol. An Outer Temple, no longer discernible, was once a tract of property owned by the Knights Templar situated outside the City boundary. The first Hall on this site was built in 1302 and the present one, which you are facing, was completed in 1573.

It is thought that William Shakespeare attended the opening night of his own play *Twelfth Night* performed here on 2 February 1601. The inside of the Hall is really worth a visit, although not always accessible to the

The impressive Middle Temple Hall gateway. LZ

public. The outstanding feature, as you view the interior of the Hall from the visitors' gallery, is the double hammer beam oak roof and screen by Edmund Plowden (1517-1584), Treasurer of the Inn and a teacher. The large and heavy 29-foot table at the end of the Hall, known as the *Bench Table*, is made from a single oak tree and was a gift from Queen Elizabeth I. Beyond it is *The Cupboard* around which the well known *moots*, or debates on theoretical or imaginary legal points, take place. On the west wall hang royal portraits and around the whole Hall is a spectacular array of Elizabethan suits of armour.

Because of the invitational system of honorary membership of The Honourable Society of the Middle Temple, which has flourished for some six centuries, many famous names are associated with the Hall: John Evelyn, Thomas More, Charles Dickens, Sir Francis Drake, Sir Walter Raleigh and Elias Ashmole, among many others.

Of Masonic Interest: **Elias Ashmole**

The culmination of Elias Ashmole's legal career was the prestigious admission to The Honourable Society of the Middle Temple, in 1657. Elias Ashmole (1617–1692) is a Masonic icon and his initiation in Warrington, then in Lancashire, on 16 October 1646 is seen as the earliest evidence of the making of a 'speculative', ie non-working, Mason in England. He had a very full and illustrious career and the Ashmolean Museum in Oxford is a witness to his achievements. By 1633 the talented 16-year-old had finished music school in his home town to find himself following a legal career in London. This served him well. Ashmole was constantly embroiled in litigation, which he invariably won. By the age of twenty-five Ashmole appears to have retired, spending the remainder of his life dedicated to academic research and success. His Masonic career is in effect non-existent outside his celebrated initiation and the visit to Masons' Hall in London recorded in his diary on 10 March 1682.

Historical Notes: The Knights Templar

The Knights Templar have maintained through the centuries an aura of mystery, legend and even romance. The powerful, monastic military Order was founded in 1118 following the first crusade and conquest of Jerusalem in 1099. Their initial humble function was to provide Christian pilgrims with protection on their way to the Holy Land. Yet within two centuries the Templars controlled lands from Scotland, across Europe and into Asia. They settled here in London on property legitimately purchased first in Holborn and later in this area. The several crusades to the Holy Land were all launched from here. At the peak of their achievements the Knights Templar were an exceedingly popular and respected group of soldier priests. It is only natural that monetary gifts from all quarters and singular privileges from monarchs and rulers were showered on them. They gradually gained great wealth and soon became international property owners and bankers. Envy, jealousy and ever-increasing criticism, mainly that their vows as Christians were being forgotten, followed and finally in October 1307, King Philip the Fair of France, in collaboration with Pope Clement V, who happened to be a Frenchman, dissolved the order and falsely accused the Templars of a series of charges including sodomy, blasphemy and heresy. The Papal Bull of 1313 formally banned the Order and the last Grand Master, Jacques De Molay (b.1244), was burned at the stake on 18 March 1314.

The Knights in London were arrested, put in the Tower and their possessions confiscated by Edward II who passed their property to the Knights Hospitaller. Following the dissolution of the monasteries by Henry VIII in 1536, all the property of the Knights Hospitaller passed to the Crown and in 1566 James I allowed lawyers, who had occupied the Inn as tenants since the late 14th century, to purchase the property. It was James I who granted the 'Benchers' ownership rights in 1608 'to serve for all time to come for the accommodation and education of the students and practitioners of laws of the realm'. They enjoy those same rights today.

Of Masonic Interest:
Order of The Knights Templar

The relationship between the Knights Templar described above and the Masonic Order, the full title of which reads 'The United Religious, Military and Masonic Orders of the Temple and of St John of Jerusalem, Palestine, Rhodes and Malta, in England and Wales and Provinces Overseas', is tenuous at best. There is no evidence of the Masonic Order before 1777 and then only as an additional degree practised within the jurisdiction of other Orders beyond the Craft. Claims of an historical connection between the medieval Knights and the present Masonic Order have been all but dismissed by modern scholars as well as members of the Order. There are still European branches of Knights Templar organisations that claim a direct descent from medieval times, believing that the Order survived in a greatly fragmented form. It is generally agreed that the Order as an organised Masonic-related entity first surfaced in France in the early 19th century, whilst a revival of the Order is manifest in the creation of the Scottish Masonic version in 1804. The debate is ongoing as to whether these events represent a new order or the rebirth of the original Knights.

In England, the growth of the Masonic Order in the mid-1800s was slow, as was the development of many other Orders under the Grand Mastership of the Duke of Sussex (1773–1843). This was peculiar to England, where the Union of the two Grand Lodges in 1813 led to the suppression of all the orders and degrees beyond the Royal Arch. From 1843, however, following the death of Sussex and his replacement by the 2nd Earl of Zetland (1795–1873), the Order began to prosper. Today some 450 Preceptories are active in England and Wales.

The bronze statue in Inner Temple is of two knights sharing a horse. LZ

STOP 8. Temple Church

DIRECTIONS: Cross over to Pump Court on your left and walk through the small archway towards the Lamb Building and up the steps into Temple Church Courtyard. **STOP (8).** You are now in the Inner Temple. Note the Pegasus winged horse symbol decorating the walls of the buildings. Stand by the column, which has at the top the bronze statue by Nicola Hicks of two knights sharing a horse. It was completed and erected in 2000. Enter the church in your own time.

Historical Notes: **The Inner Temple Area**

The layout of the whole area reflected the traditional four-fold division of the Knights, namely Squires, Armourers, Priests and other lay members of the Order. The Knights and Squires lived around the cloisters facing the south side of the Temple Church, the current Inner Temple Hall, which is in view and was built in 1955 by Sir Hubert Worthington (1886–1963). It replaced the 1868 Gothic building by Sydney Smirke (1798–1877). The clergy lived to the east of the church, where the Master's house now lies, and the lay brothers' hall was situated where Elm and Pump Courts now are. Smirke's building was badly damaged by enemy action in 1941, and some forty-five thousand books lost when the adjoining library received a direct hit. The new library, completed by Sir Edward Maufe (1883–1974) in 1956, now houses some ninety-five thousand books. Some very well-known and famous people have been residents of the Inner Temple. Outside Crown Office Row is a plaque to Charles Lamb (1775–1834) and another nearby records that William Makepeace Thackeray (1811–1863) lived here. No 1 Inner Temple Lane is dedicated to Dr Samuel Johnson (1709-1784) and in Hare Court are the Chambers of the infamous Lord Chief Justice Jeffreys (1648–1689), the original 'Hanging Judge'.

Historical Notes: **Temple Church**

Heraclius (d.1191), Patriarch of Jerusalem, in the presence of King Henry II (reigned 1154–1189), consecrated the Temple Church in 1185, modelled on the Holy Sepulchre in Jerusalem. Its shape and form remain identical to the original though many repairs have been made over the centuries. On entering the church through the side south door, turn left and stand in the centre of the round. Six Purbeck marble pillars hanging almost like iron drapery surround you. They help carry the weight of the vaulting. Along the edge are numerous grotesque carved stone heads, the handiwork of the stonemasons.

On the ground are 10 full-size effigies of crusaders in armour. Central is the figure of William the Marshal (1146–1219), the Earl of Pembroke, Rector of England under Henry III, and his seven sons surround him. The

The Temple Church is modelled on the Holy Sepulchre, Jerusalem. LZ

On the ground in the Temple Church are full-size effigies. LZ other marked effigies are of 'A Member of the Ross Family — 14th century' and of Geoffrey de Mandeville, 1st Earl of Essex, the lawless Baron who died in 1144 with an arrow through his head. Because he was excommunicated for murdering monks, he could not be buried on holy ground, in spite of being a Knights Templar, until the Pope had absolved him. Meanwhile he was sealed in a lead coffin and hung from a tree in Holborn until he could be buried in the Temple Church. The effigies were transported to their present location in 1841, having until then been situated outside the Temple. Opposite the entrance to the church, on the north side is the penitential cell, visible though not accessible. The cell, used to punish disobedient members of the order, measures only five feet by three feet allowing the prisoner neither to stand nor lie down and was known as *Little Ease*. Its best-known victim was Walter le Batchelor, the Grand Preceptor of Ireland, who starved to death in the cell in 1301 for disobeying the Master of the Temple.

At the west end is the original entrance to the church – a graceful Norman doorway, where abandoned babies were often left on the steps in the hope that the Templars would look after them, which they always did, giving them the surname 'Templar'. The Temple Church is one of the very few round churches remaining in England. The rectangular choir was added in 1220. The church is shared equally by the Middle and Inner Temples. The pews face the aisle and members of the Inner Temple sit in the south, whilst those of the Middle Temple sit in the north.

The church is generally open Wednesdays to Sundays from 1.00pm to 4.00pm. Visitors may attend the Sunday Service at 11.15am. Further information can be obtained by calling 020 7353 3470.

Of Masonic Interest: **The Da Vinci Code**

The Temple Church has recently been publicised in Dan Brown's *The Da Vinci Code*. The book has been described as a combination of myth and reality or

Filming Dan Brown's The Da Vinci Code in the Temple area. LZ.

believable fiction, an intellectual and fact-based suspense thriller. It covers a huge range of fascinating subjects such as renaissance art, theological heresy and theoretical mathematics as well as Freemasonry, the Knights Templar and other esoteric, mystic and Catholic orders. The key claim behind the story is that Christianity is based upon a Big Lie, namely that the true worship of the Divine Feminine was suppressed by the myth of the divinity of Christ. The book claims that Jesus Christ was married to Mary Magdalene who bore His child. Jesus had intended Mary Magdalene to lead the church after His death, but Peter objected and Mary Magdalene and her child were exiled to Gaul, taking with them the Holy Grail. In *The Da Vinci Code* the Knights Templar are implicated in dozens of mysteries, and rumoured to be the guardians of the Holy Grail and keepers of secret esoteric knowledge. The tale and trail near the end in the Temple Church, which since the publication of the book has become a Mecca to the *aficionados* of Dan Brown stories.

The Norman gate entrance to the Temple Church. LZ

STOP 9. Prince Henry's Room

DIRECTIONS: Exit Temple Church and turn sharply to your right. Leave the Inner Temple area by walking along the left-hand side (west) of the church past Dr Johnson's Building. Note the exterior of the Norman gate entrance into Temple Church as you walk by. Exit by the north end gateway back into Fleet Street, opposite Chancery Lane. **STOP (9).** The half-timber work of the gateway comprises Prince Henry's Room and the Pepys Museum above the gateway.

Museum Notes:
Prince Henry's Room and Pepys Museum
The building above the gateway, at 17 Fleet Street, was built in 1610 and survived both the Great Fire of 1666 as well as Second World War bombing. The exceptional plaster ceiling on the first-floor room is named after the Prince of Wales, Prince Henry, who died of typhoid at the young age of 18. As the elder son of James I, he became the Duke of Cornwall, and he used this room as an office. The room, with its decorative plasterwork and delicate wood panelling, houses a collection of memorabilia relating to the diarist Samuel Pepys (1633–1703). Whilst working as Secretary to the Admiralty, Pepys chronicled, *inter alia*, the Great Plague of 1665 and the Great Fire of London of 1666. Although located in a private office building, the Museum room is open to the public, free of charge, Monday to Friday from 11.00am to 2.00pm. For further information call 020 8294 1158.

The building above the gateway of No 17 Fleet Street was built in 1610. LZ

Four Lodges met at the Goose and Gridiron. Guildhall

STOP 10. Mitre Tavern

DIRECTIONS: Turn right along Fleet Street towards St Paul's and after about 50 yards further on stop at No 37 Fleet Street, now 'Messrs. Hoare Bankers AD1672', straight opposite the church of St Dunstan in the West. **STOP (10).** On the wall by the entrance is another blue plaque, which reads: 'Site of the Mitre Tavern'.

Of Masonic Interest: **Antients v Moderns**

The Mitre Tavern, which was situated at what is now 37 Fleet Street, was another classic Masonic meeting place with one exceptional circumstance. It served to accommodate lodge meetings of both the Antient and Modern Grand Lodges. How unusual an event this is can be appreciated when looking at the origins of the great conflict that lasted the best part of six decades.

It is now a well-recorded fact that organised Freemasonry began in London on 24 June 1717, founded by four lodges meeting at the Goose and Gridiron. By the middle of the 18th century, however, Freemasonry began to go into a decline and on 17 July 1751 five 'Irish' lodges consecrated the *Antients* Grand Lodge in direct competition, if not conflict, with the Premier Grand Lodge of 1717, which was soon dubbed 'The Moderns'. These incongruous terms have remained in use to this day. Thus from July 1751, two Grand Lodges in England ran at loggerheads until the final agreements from which, finally, the United Grand Lodge of England emerged in December 1813. It seems, therefore, quite extraordinary that rival lodges belonging to the Premier or 'Moderns' Grand Lodge of 1717 and those of the 'Antients' of 1751 met at this venue. The Lodge of Antiquity number 2, one of the four founding lodges of the premier Grand Lodge that met at the Goose and Gridiron, moved to The Mitre in Fleet Street in 1769. It continued to meet there until 1781 when it moved to Freemasons' Hall in Great Queen Street. During this same period in 1778 the Antients Lodge of Hope number 4, which had been meeting at the Sun Tavern in Ludgate, moved to the same Mitre Tavern. Under these circumstances it seems almost logical that the short-lived and rebel 'Grand Lodge of England South of the River Trent', should also have met here. Chartered by the Grand Lodge of All England in York on 29 March 1779, it collapsed in 1787. The brethren frequenting The Mitre followed in distinguished footsteps. Records show that among many famed individuals, William Shakespeare and Samuel Johnson were both patrons of the old Mitre Tavern.

Historical Notes: Taverns

By the time David Saunders introduced coffee into England from Turkey in 1652, taverns had been around for many centuries. In Roman times taverns were placed within the City gates to provide for travellers. This practice continued into the Middle Ages and was emulated by the ecclesiastical bodies, most notably in the City, the four St Botolph churches: Aldgate, Aldersgate, Bishopsgate and Billingsgate, the first three of which are still today associated with giving relief and sanctuary to the homeless. The concept of the tavern has always been — and still is, in the guise of a public house — a culture in its own right. Antiquated rules and regulations governing the drinking trade are found in the Orders of the Corporation and Acts of Parliament dating from the reign of Edward III (1312-1377). They particularly relate to the penalties imposed for adulteration of wine. A limit on the number of taverns within the City was enacted in 1552 'for the avoiding many inconveniences, much evil rule and common resort to misruled persons ...' By 1688 there were 40 taverns in London and three in Westminster. Several taverns had entertainment, in addition to the companionship to be found in groups of familiar faces drinking together.

In the 17th and 18th centuries, because of the shortage of coinage in England brought about by the war effort, both taverns and coffee house owners issued their own redeemable tokens. So did other tradesmen with coins made from brass, pewter and copper, and sometimes leather, bearing the issuer's name, address, or some reference to their trade. In taverns the most popular token was the halfpenny.

Of Masonic Interest: Sketchley Token

The only known examples of a monetary Masonic token were issued in 1792. An entrepreneurial Freemason, James Sketchley of Birmingham, was responsible. An auctioneer, printer and publisher, he had several confrontations with Masonic authority but his devotion to the Craft allowed him to overcome them. In June 1792 Sketchley was appointed the first Provincial Grand Secretary of Warwickshire, the zenith of an outstanding career, which came to an unfortunate end. An entry dated 27 December 1796 in the minute book of St John's Lodge at Henley-in-Arden (which James Sketchley had helped to consecrate in 1792) includes the following entry:

Financial trouble led Sketchley to issue halfpenny tokens. YB

'A motion being made by our W M on account of a letter received from our brother Sketchley informing us, that he being in great distress, a subscription was proposed… which amounted to One pound four shillings . . .'

It may have been financial trouble that led Sketchley to issue his halfpenny tokens, which saw circulation as currency and were used for trade.

The design on the obverse of the token was adopted from the title page of *The Freemason's Magazine*. The coat of arms on the reverse is that of the Premier Grand Lodge of England. The aspect of interest to collectors is the variation in the edge readings on each token. This is also a factor in establishing the original use of the tokens. The halfpenny token was used as small change by some publicans in the meeting-places of Masonic lodges. Thus the edge-reading 'Halfpenny payable at the Black Horse Tower Hill' is evidence of such use. The tokens saw circulation in London, Dublin, Cork, Derry, Lancaster and Bristol. The words 'Masonic' and 'halfpenny' appear on several tokens, and Sketchley's name, spelt in various ways, is also to be encountered. The earliest token was issued in 1794, although the legend on the obverse states '24 NOV 1790'. The date refers to the installation of The Prince of Wales, later King George IV, as Grand Master. The monetary halfpenny Masonic token was issued to commemorate this event. For a Freemason to issue a monetary token, and to choose a Masonic event of important significance for its design, was both logical and practical. In September 1794 the following advertisement appeared in *The Freemason's Magazine*:

'Masonic Tokens
In the course of the past month, some copper pieces newly struck from a die, which appears to be executed in a stile superior to any of the Provincial Coins at present in circulation, came to the hands of the Proprietor of this MAGAZINE. On inspection they appear to be called MASONIC

TOKENS, and to have been invented by a Brother JAMES SKETCHLEY, of BIRMINGHAM . . . It would appear that many persons have been content to receive them in change as halfpence currency.'

James Sketchley died in Poughkeepsie, New York, in August 1801 but curiously there is no record of his travel to or stay in the United States of America.

The site of the City of London's first coffee house, the 'Pasque Rose'. LZ

Historical Notes: **Advent of the coffee house**

England's first coffee house appeared in 1650 in Oxford and in 1652 the City of London's first shop opened in St. Michael's Alley, Cornhill. It was called the Pasque Rose and the site is there today.

The popularity of coffee houses spread like wildfire. Before the introduction of coffee many people drank beer or wine for breakfast. Coffee houses soon became multi-functional premises serving, for instance, as postal and news distribution centres, successfully competing with the rather inadequate national postal services. The competition generated by this new phenomenon of the coffee house naturally antagonised tavern owners, innkeepers and vintners who, as early as 1673, petitioned against tea, coffee, brandy '. . . as the use of these newer drinks might interfere with that of the native Barley, Malt and Wheat'. The tavern owners and innkeepers spread false rumours in an attempt to dissuade patrons from attending coffee houses. They claimed that roasting coffee beans was dangerous both to health and as a fire hazard. All this was to no avail. By 1700, there were over 2,000 coffee houses in London alone. Although initially coffee houses served only coffee and non-alcoholic beverages, by the 1750s alcoholic drinks were introduced and their popularity increased. When the taverns in the City closed their doors at 9.00pm customers moved to the coffee houses. As with taverns, a series of strict rules governed conduct in coffee houses. Gambling was effectively banned with prohibition on the use of playing cards and dice. A wager was limited to five shillings. A plaque in one of the coffee houses stated:

'He that shall any quarrel begin
Shall give each man a dish to atone his sin
On sacred things, let none presume to touch,
Nor profane scriptures,
Nor saucily wrong Affairs of state
With an irreverent tongue.
Let mirth be innocent.'

Whilst taverns maintained their image as popular drinking and socialising venues, the coffee house developed an element of intellect, which served it well. It became a great social leveller. At a time when England was under strict Puritan rule, here the debating of political and literary ideas was encouraged, creating the first true cradle of democracy. They became fashionable meeting places for businessmen. The best-known instance in 1688 is that of Edward Bransby who had five watches stolen. He placed an advertisement in the London Gazette offering a guinea reward claimable at Edward Lloyd's Coffee House in Tower Street. As a result, insurance underwriters began to meet at Lloyd's Coffee House to make themselves available to potential insurers. It was the start of Lloyd's of London, the largest insurance organisation the world was to know. Coffee houses also became the favourite venue for such famous writers as James Boswell, Jonathan Swift and Daniel Defoe. They would mingle here with men from all levels of society: quacks and impostors, tradesmen as well as the nobility. Coffee houses became the respectable venue for free discussion and the exchange of ideas and opinions that had never before existed in England. Through the coffee house, leaflets and pamphlets on every conceivable theme were distributed, disseminating views and information that influenced London's society. The coffee and teahouse had the greatest influence in the development of a free press.

Of Masonic Interest: **1698 Pamphlet**

In 1698, nearly two decades before the formation of the Premier Grand Lodge, a small-size dated pamphlet was distributed in the streets of the City and the coffee houses. The leaflet, headed 'To All Godly People, in the Citie of London', is the earliest overt evidence of antagonism towards the Craft. The text reads as follows:

'Having thought it needful to warn you/ of the Mischiefs and Evils practiced/ in the Sight of GOD by those called / Freed Masons, I say take Care lest their Cer- / emonies and secret Swearings take hold of / you; and be weary that none cause you to err / from Godliness. For this Devlish sect of / Men are Meeters in secret which swear against / all without their Following. They are the / Anti Christ which was to come leading / Men from Fear of GOD. For how should / Men meet in secret Places and with secret / Signs taking Care that none observe them to / do the Work of GOD; are not these the Ways / of Evil-doers?

'Knowing how that GOD observeth pri-/ villy them that sit in Darkness they shall be/ smitten and the Secrets of their Hearts layed / bare. Mingle not among this corrupt People/ lest you be found so at the World's Conflag- / ration.'

Very little information on the circumstances under which the pamphlet was issued is known. The time period and context, however, are of relevance. Freemasonry is here considered an evil institution because of its secret signs and meeting places. The oaths referred to in the pamphlet do not correspond to the obligations we take today. What is clear is that at the time of the distribution of the leaflet, Masonic oaths and secret meeting places were considered to be anti-social. The implication, by the very existence of this leaflet, is that Freemasonry in 1698 was of sufficient consequence to justify such an attack. From a viewpoint of classification only, the 1698 pamphlet is seen as a religious attack on Freemasonry. It was the first in a long series of such attacks.

STOP 11. Gough Square

DIRECTIONS: Continue along Fleet Street to the second set of pedestrian lights and cross to the other side. Turn right towards St Paul's Cathedral and take the third lane on your left, following the signpost to Dr Johnson's House. Walk past the blue plaque on the wall until you reach Gough Square. **STOP (11).**

Historical Notes: **Samuel Johnson**
The house at 17 Gough Square, Samuel Johnson's home for more than a decade, is one of the few residential houses of its age still surviving in the City. Built in 1700, it was the home and workplace of Samuel Johnson from 1748 to 1759. Here he compiled the first comprehensive English dictionary. Now restored to its original condition, the house contains panelled rooms, a pine staircase, and a collection of period furniture, prints and portraits. The

appointed curator of the building enjoys a special privilege. He or she is allowed to live in the quaint cottage adjoining the Museum. Dr Samuel Johnson was born on 18 September 1709 in Lichfield, Staffordshire. His early life was beset by ill health, his eyesight and hearing in particular being very poor. He was educated at Lichfield Grammar School and Pembroke College, Oxford, but was obliged to leave without a degree in 1735, unable to pay his tuition fees. Johnson married Elizabeth Porter, a widow more than 20 years his senior, and struggled to support himself through journalism. He wrote his two best-known poems, *London* and *The Vanity of Human Wishes*, before being commissioned to write a dictionary by a syndicate of printers. He rented 17 Gough Square, and with the help of his six amanuenses, compiled the dictionary in the garret. After the death of his beloved wife in 1752, his Jamaican servant, Francis Barber, joined him. It was only in 1762, when George III granted him an annual pension of £300 that Johnson was able to live more comfortably. At this time he became friends with a young Scottish lawyer named James Boswell, who was to become Johnson's biographer. Despite his age, in 1773 Johnson set out with Boswell for a three-month tour of the Scottish Highlands and Islands. Two years later, he was granted an honorary degree by Oxford University. He died in 1784, and is buried at Westminster Abbey.

The statue to 'Hodge' opposite the house reflects Johnson's special affection for his cat. He was even known to feed it with oysters, which he himself would fetch from the local market. Jon Bickley, the English sculptor and a lover of cats and other four-footed animals, executed the sculpture. Hodge sits patiently atop a bronze version of the Dictionary. The statue was unveiled in 1997 in the presence of the Lord Mayor of London. 'I made Hodge about shoulder high for the average adult', the sculptor explains, 'which is just about right for putting an arm around it.'

17 Gough Square was Samuel Johnson's home. LZ

Hodge sits patiently atop a bronze version of the Dictionary. LZ

Of Masonic Interest: **James Boswell**

Although Samuel Johnson was not a Freemason he would have been exposed to Freemasonry through the close relationship he enjoyed with James Boswell (1740–1795) who became Johnson's right-hand man, best friend and biographer. A Scottish man-of-letters, lawyer and essayist, Boswell is best known for his two-volume biography *The Life Of Samuel Johnson, LL.D*, published in 1791, seven years after Johnson's death. They met in May 1763 and became life-long friends. Boswell recorded in great detail Johnson's words and activities during a relatively short period. James Boswell was born in Edinburgh, the son of Alexander Boswell, Lord Auchinleck, who was a judge in the Supreme Court of Scotland. He went to the University of Edinburgh in 1753, where he studied arts and law. In 1766, Boswell was admitted to the bar in Scotland and practised law in Edinburgh for twenty years before moving to London, where he died on 19 May 1795.

Boswell was an active Freemason. He served as Master of Canongate Kilwinning Lodge for two terms. In February 1777 he was made an honorary member of Edinburgh Lodge, having been appointed Depute Grand Master for Scotland in 1776 for a two-year term. He declined to be nominated for Grand Master. Many other members of his family were also Freemasons. His son, Sir Alexander Boswell (1775–1822), a Scottish songwriter and printer and also Master of Mother Kilwinning Lodge, composed many Masonic songs including *The Mother Lodge, Kilwinning*. Johnson and Boswell attended a Masonic funeral at Rochester with Johnson's admirer and good friend, Bennett Langton. Boswell recorded that Dr Johnson, having witnessed the Masonic funeral procession, was impressed by the solemn music being played on French horns, and said, 'This is the first time that I have ever been affected by musical sounds',

adding that the impression made upon him 'was of a melancholy kind'.

Museum Notes: **Johnson's House**

Dr Johnson's House is open to the public throughout the year, from Monday to Saturday. The opening hours are 11.00am to 5.30pm, May to September, and 11.00am to 5.00pm, October to April. The house is closed on Sundays and Bank Holidays.

STOP 12. Cheshire Cheese Tavern

DIRECTIONS: Walk through the archway to the left of the statue of Hodge, the cat, into Gunpowder Square. Wine Office Court faces you and extends to your right. Turn right toward the Cheshire Cheese sign visible less than 50 yards ahead. Wine Office Court derives its name from the tax offices situated here, where payment for wine and spirit licences was made in the 17th and 18th centuries. **STOP (12)** at the rails opposite the entrance to the Cheshire Cheese Tavern.

Historical Notes: **Cheshire Cheese**

'Ye Olde Cheshire Cheese' is one of the few taverns that can genuinely call itself 'old'. Several parts of the original building are still intact as they were in 1667, when the tavern was rebuilt after the Great Fire of 1666. These premises are the nearest we are likely to encounter to the Goose and Gridiron which would have looked like this in 1717 at the time Grand Lodge was formed. The Cheshire Cheese dates much further back to the 16th century and the board on display lists fifteen monarchs whose reigns it has survived. The interior is dark and wooden, and an enchanting warren of corridors and narrow staircases leads to several bars and dining rooms on five levels, three below ground and two above. The quaint tavern retains the early style and arrangement of fireplaces in each of the several small rooms furnished with tables and benches. The famous small

'Ye Olde Cheshire Cheese' is a famous and popular tavern off Fleet Street. LZ ground-floor bar room is decorated with black timber, including the panelled ceiling. An open fire gives the room a special atmosphere. The portrait above the fireplace is that of a waiter who began to work at the Cheshire Cheese in 1829. Until recently on the shelf behind the bar, a leather-bound visitors' book containing the names and autographs of hundreds of dignitaries, prime ministers, ambassadors and peers, academics and artists, was available to view. It is now stored away for safety and posterity. Dr Johnson's well-publicised and regular attendance at the Cheshire Cheese made the tavern a place of pilgrimage for many 19th century literary figures. Mark Twain, Thackeray and Charles Dickens are among those who patronised this most famous and popular tavern off Fleet Street.

Of Masonic Interest: Lodge Meeting Places

Organised Freemasonry had its origins in the Goose and Gridiron where the first Grand Lodge in the world was formed on 22 June 1717. Although, with the advent of nobility in our midst just a few years later, lodge meetings were sometimes held in the private homes and mansions of members of the aristocracy, the majority of the lodges continued to meet in taverns and a few coffee houses. The 18th century tavern was an ideal meeting place for Freemasons who congregated in an atmosphere of good fellowship, fun and happiness. Frequently the publican owner of the tavern was made a Freemason, often acting as the Tyler. Grand Lodge discouraged this practice. The well-known engraved Lists of Lodges published since 1723, leading to the current familiar *Year Book*, identified each lodge with a quaint copper-engraved illustration of the tavern or coffee house sign where the lodge met. Famous artists were commissioned to execute the engravings: John Pine, Emanuel Bowen and Benjamin Cole, all Freemasons. By the time Freemasonry began to spread at the end of the 17th century, the coffee house had been on the scene for well over half a century, yet Freemasons showed a preference for the tavern, probably because of the availability of alcohol, this, notwithstanding the high social mixture and more sophisticated atmosphere of the coffee house.

Of the 30 lodges in London in 1726, only two met at a coffee house. In the next 150 years, some 400 new lodges were consecrated, only 34 of them in coffee houses. The Royal Inverness Lodge, No. 648, the first lodge warranted by the newly established United Grand Lodge of England, in 1814, was the last lodge to be consecrated in a coffee house, the Gray's Inn in Holborn. At the start of the 19th century, the establishment of Masonic Halls and especially Freemasons' Hall, which incidentally began its life as a tavern in its own right, changed the meeting habits of most lodges. Interestingly today some lodges still meet in public houses, which are particularly popular with Schools and Lodges of Instruction. Freemasonry generally attracted support from the gentry, merchants and the middle classes, and members were often affiliated to other clubs and societies of the time. It should be noted that, unlike Europe, where Freemasons had to meet in secret because the Craft was suppressed and attacked, here in England Freemasons operated openly, allowing them to meet publicly in taverns and coffee houses.

The entrance hall of the Daily Express building is displayed when the curtains are drawn open. LZ

STOP 13. Fleet Street

DIRECTIONS: Exit the Cheshire Cheese and turn to your left, leaving Wine Office Court into Fleet Street. Turn left and walk 200 yards to the Daily Express building at number 120-129 on the corner of Shoe Lane. **STOP (13).**

Historical Notes: **Fleet Street**

When William Caxton died in 1491 his apprentice, Wynkyn de Worde (d.1535) took over the business and moved the print shop from Westminster to the churchyard of St Bride's in Fleet Street. It was an ideal spot for a printer, near Bridewell Palace frequented by the nobility, the Temple where lawyers dwelt and worked, and St Paul's Cathedral, the courtyard already established as a meeting place for Londoners. De Worde knew that only lawyers and the nobility could afford books.

In 1702 the first newspaper, the *Daily Courant*, was published in Ludgate Circus and *The Times*, which survives to this day, saw the light of day in 1785 in Fleet Street. The Daily Express Building you are standing in front of was commissioned by William Maxwell Aitken (1879–1964), Lord Beaverbrook, the highly successful newspaper baron and owner of the most widely read newspaper in the world. The premises were custom-built by Sir Owen Williams (1890–1969). The frontage is black Vitrolite transparent glass, set in chromium strips.

The entrance hall, which is displayed when the curtains are drawn open, has been described as 'luxurious and sensational in the art deco style'. It today houses the offices of Goldman Sachs, the American brokers who are also the proprietors of the adjoining Peterborough

Court, the former home of *The Daily Telegraph*, owned and run in the 1930s by William Hesketh Lever, the 1st Lord Leverhulme (1851–1925), who, incidentally, was Provincial Grand Master of Cheshire. The 1929 architects were Elcock and Sutcliffe. These and other major national newspapers were all in great competition with each other, all being printed in this same area until the move to Canary Wharf from 1985 onwards. The imposing building at No 85, across the street from where you stand, housed the international news agency Reuters. They were the last to move to Canary Wharf, in 2005. Paul Julius Reuter (1816–1899) founded the agency in 1850, well known in those days for flying flocks of pigeons to deliver news of stock market prices from Aachen to Brussels. The 1920s building is by Sir Edwin Lutyens (1869–1944) and, like many of the buildings in the City, is constructed of heavily rusticated cladding of Dorset's Portland stone.

The area has changed dramatically from the days when pressmen spent their time late into the night, drinking and chatting in any one of the hundreds of pubs, coffee houses and restaurants, waiting for the first edition of their respective newspaper. That very special atmosphere has not been recreated in the computerised and digital world of Canary Wharf. It is lost for ever.

Of Masonic Interest: **Masonic Press**

The press in 1717 totally ignored the establishment of Grand Lodge at the Goose and Gridiron on 24 June. It was simply not a newsworthy event. Nevertheless the first mention of Freemasonry in a newspaper pre-dated Grand Lodge. It can be found in number 26 of *The Tatler* for Tuesday 7 June 1709. It is in the form of an anonymous letter addressed to Isaac Bickerstaff, pseudonym of Richard Steele, who established *The Tatler* on 12 April 1709. The relevant paragraph reads:

'. . . Some of them I have heard calling to one another . . . by the Names of, Betty, Nelly, and so forth. You see them accost each other with effeminate Airs: They have their Signs and Tokens like Free-Masons: They rail at Womankind; . .'

The use of newspapers by the Masonic fraternity itself, however, was not long in coming. All kinds of announcements by the Premier Grand Lodge became increasingly frequent. *The Daily Courant* of 5 September 1719, for instance, has an announcement stating that '. . . Master Masons in & about London are desired to meet some of their Brethren at the Vine Tavern on the Thursday'. A series of announcements in the years following the formation of Grand Lodge gives details of the admission of various personalities into the Society of Free-Masons. *Read's Weekly Journal* of 1 December 1722 has the first-ever appearance of the *Enter'd 'Prentice's Song* composed by the actor and Freemason, Mathew Birkhead. The song was later included in Anderson's first Book of Constitutions of 1723. The first hints of antagonism towards the Craft also appeared in *The London Journal* on 15 February 1722 when it was announced that '. . . a treatise is likely soon to appear . . . to prove, that the Gypsies are a Society of much longer standing than that of Free-Masons'. This was followed by the more blatant attack, the first exposure of Masonic ritual, which appeared in the *Flying Post* on 11–13 April 1723, commonly referred to as *A Mason's Examination*.

St Bride's Churchyard is entered through St Bride's Avenue. LZ

STOP 14. St Bride's Church

DIRECTIONS: The little island in the middle of Fleet Street will help you cross to the other side. There is no pedestrian crossing at this point. Enter St Bride's Churchyard through St Bride's Avenue. Walk through the main gate into the courtyard. **STOP (14).**

Historical Notes: **St Bride's Church**

St Bride's Church, known as St Bridget's until the 19th century, refers to the Irish St Bridget born in AD453. The word Bridewell is derived from the fact that until the 19th century there was a water spring at the top of the hill where the church is situated. St Bride's has become well known because its spire has inspired the design for wedding cakes since the late 18th century. The name is totally coincidental. A pastry cook named William Rich (1755–1811), whose bakery was at 3 Ludgate Hill, made tiered wedding cakes copying the church spire and the fashion became a tradition.

There has been a church on this site since AD900 and the crypt contains the remnants of a Roman pavement. It is now considered one of Wren's most classical and beautiful churches, rebuilt and completed in 1675 following its destruction in the Great Fire. The Portland stone tower and steeple is designed in diminishing octagons and was erected in 1701. The steeple, which rises 234 feet, was intended to be seen from both the Fleet River and the Thames. It was rebuilt after severe damage during the Second World War when only the tower remained intact. Whilst rebuilding took place, some important and fascinating archaeological discoveries were made. It is now known that at least five churches have stood on this site. In spite of the outflow of the newspaper trade to Canary Wharf, St Bride's continues as the 'Journalist's Church' and the 'Printer's Cathedral'. One chapel is dedicated to reporters — in the widest sense of the word — who have lost their lives on assignment anywhere in the world, including the recent Gulf Wars.

Museum Notes: **St Bride's Crypt**

The crypt is a museum displaying a Roman tessellated pavement, Saxon remains and an extraordinary collection of skulls. The diarist Samuel Pepys (1633–1703) was born one street away and he and his eight brothers and sisters were all baptised in the church. His brother Tom is buried in the crypt. The church is open to the public free of charge at regular opening times.

STOP 15. Fleet River

DIRECTIONS: Exit the gates of St Bride's Church and return to Fleet Street turning right towards St Paul's. Cross New Bridge Street at the lights and turn right toward Blackfriars Bridge. **STOP (15)** at the base of the steps at Pilgrim Street.

Historical Note: **The Fleet River**

The street you have just crossed covers what was the Fleet River, known also as Holbourne, which still runs underneath the road. It originates some eight miles to the north from springs on Hampstead Heath and exits at Blackfriars Bridge, just to your left. The water is directed to reservoirs in Hampstead Ponds whence it continues to the Thames. Until about 1740 it consisted of navigable waters with docks set up at what is now Farringdon Street. Centuries earlier than that, however, the Fleet had already become a sewer. Its value as a navigable waterway for light shipping was lost by the 16th century, because it became shallow and slow running and was totally polluted. From 1652 attempts were made by the authorities to clean the Fleet River and prohibit the dumping of waste but to no avail. Following the Great Fire, proposals by Sir Christopher Wren to rebuild the Fleet and widen the banks with broad embankments were only partly fulfilled. The lower part of the river was dredged and widened into a canal, completed in 1674, whilst the river north of Holborn to the City was covered over.

The new Fleet Canal failed. Guildhall

The new Fleet Canal, however, failed. Commercial traffic never used it and it soon reverted to a dump for raw sewage and rubbish. In 1766 the whole of the Fleet was arched and remains to this day part of London's underground rainwater sewer.

The steps at Pilgrim Street, looking towards St Paul's. LZ

STOP 16. St Paul's and the Goose & Gridiron

DIRECTIONS: Climb the steps behind you and walk past Pageantmaster Court. Turn right at Ludgate Broadway and left into Carter Lane. Walk to the top, passing the King's Wardrobe on your right, and turn left at Dean's Court past the Bishop of London's Mansion.

At the main road leading to Ludgate Hill, St Paul's Cathedral looms enormous and proud before you. Turn left to the crossing and make your way to the bottom step of St Paul's Cathedral.

Follow the lowest step to your left until you reach the columns of Paternoster Square **STOP (16)**. You stand at what was the entrance to the Goose and Gridiron Tavern. The plaque commemorating the formation of Grand Lodge in 1717 is on your right at the end of the row.

Historical Notes: St Paul's Cathedral
The first St Paul's Cathedral on this site was built by the Saxons in AD604 and a cathedral has dominated the London skyline ever since. The present building by Sir Christopher Wren is the fourth on the same site and was built between 1675 and 1710 following the Great Fire of 1666. It is one of

St Paul's Cathedral looms enormous and proud. LZ

The entrance to the Goose and Gridiron Tavern. LZ

interior is 'most dreary, dingy and undevotional'. The result was the magnificent mosaics placed here in the mid-19th century. The organ still in use today dates to 1695 and was used by Felix Mendelssohn (1809–1847), who dedicated one of his compositions to the cathedral. Behind the High Altar is the American Memorial Chapel, which was a part of the cathedral damaged during the Second World War. It was built as a gesture of gratitude from the people of Britain to the American dead of the Second World War.

The cathedral, as the spiritual centre of the whole of England, has had major events throughout history held in its impressive interior: the funerals of Lord Nelson, the Duke of Wellington and Sir Winston Churchill; the Jubilee celebrations for Queen Victoria and King George V and more recently the wedding of Charles, Prince of Wales, to Lady Diana Spencer and the Golden Jubilee of Her Majesty the Queen, among many other events. Relevant to the City is the blessing of the new Lord Mayor, given by the Bishop of London at the end of the first leg of the Lord Mayor's Show on the first Saturday in November each year.

the largest cathedrals in England and Wren's masterpiece. He fashioned the façade with two tiers of paired Corinthian columns and framed them between towers. His genius came into play with the creation of a completely new architectural feature, the enormous dome, which could not possibly be accommodated on the inside of the cathedral. The solution was a double-dome structure, a small inner one and a larger one outside with a brick cone in between the two. It satisfied the requirements of the City authorities, who wanted this to be an everlasting and prestigious status symbol for the City. The first service in the cathedral took place before its completion, in 1679.

Inside the cathedral, the crypt has medieval effigies and fragments of stone that are a relic of the past. The beautiful wrought-iron gates, which separate the quire from the ambulatory, were executed in 1700 by Jean Tijou (fl.1689–c1711), the French contemporary designer of ironwork. Queen Victoria is on record as not liking St Paul's. She is reported to have commented that the

Of Masonic Interest: **Goose and Gridiron**

The Goose and Gridiron tavern, known as The Mitre before the Great Fire, has gone down in Masonic history as the site of the foundation of the first Grand Lodge in the world on 24 June 1717. When it was rebuilt after the fire it was named 'The Lyre' and, because of its musical association, it adopted Apollo's lyre surmounted by a swan as its sign. This was the origin of the tavern being mis-named the Goose and Gridiron. Here four London lodges gathered to launch organised Freemasonry and elect their first Grand Master, Anthony Sayer (1672-1742), Gentleman. Freemasonry has not looked back since. In 1995 the Goose and Gridiron Society was founded. A year later a well-supported application was made to the Corporation of London for a blue plaque to

The redeveloped Paternoster Square. LZ

The plaque commemorates the formation of Grand Lodge. LZ

STOP 17. Return Of The Temple Bar

DIRECTIONS: A few yards from the plaque is the great gateway: the recently restored old Temple Bar. **STOP (17)**

Historical Notes: **Return of the Temple Bar**

In 1984 the Temple Bar Trust successfully applied for permission to remove the Temple Bar from its location at Theobald's Park, Hertfordshire, and re-erect it at the new Paternoster Square in the vicinity of St Paul's Cathedral. It took almost 20 years to raise the funds, the target being finally reached in 2003. Thus the Temple Bar was dismantled and the 2,650 numbered stones were cleaned before being re-assembled on the present site. It now forms an elegant pedestrian gateway connecting the ancient St Paul's Cathedral with the modern redeveloped Paternoster Square. All the original features, if somewhat worn, are there. The four royal statues of Charles I, Charles II, James I and Anne of Denmark

be erected on the site. The plaque was formally unveiled on 24 June 1997.

Unfortunately, the building on which the plaque was to be placed was due to be demolished in the redevelopment of Paternoster Square. Thus there was a second unveiling of the blue plaque on 15 June 2005 by the then Lord Mayor, Alderman V. W. Bro Michael Savery, which now records for posterity the site of the beginnings of the greatest worldwide fraternal organisation.

The old Temple Bar has been recently restored. LZ

carved by John Bushnell have been restored and returned to the four niches on the main elevations of the structure. The Temple Bar Trust was established in 1976 with the specific intention of returning the Temple Bar to the City of London. The late Sir Hugh Wontner, Lord Mayor in 1974, established the Trust. Ten years later the Trust became owners of the Temple Bar and permission was granted for the removal of the Bar from Theobald's Park. At 11.00am on 10 November 2004, Alderman Robert Finch, Lord Mayor, unveiled the commemorative plaque and pushed the 1.2-ton gates open, formally returning the Temple Bar to the City. The Lady Mayoress, Mr Alderman and Sheriff John Hughesdon and Mrs Hughesdon, members of the Court of Common Council, 350 invited guests and many interested spectators witnessed this historic event.

Of Masonic Interest: **Temple Bar Lodge**

One evening in late 1877 ten London Freemasons held a meeting in the Strand, and as they were leaving they happened to see the old Temple Bar Monument being readied for removal. The sight of this so moved the petitioners that they decided to name their new lodge Temple Bar in honour of Sir Christopher Wren's architectural masterpiece. Temple Bar Lodge No 1728 was consecrated on 4 January 1878. At the second regular meeting of the lodge a letter from the City Architect, W Bro Horace Jones, who had been Master of Jerusalem Lodge No 197 in 1867, was read stating that he had been instructed by the City Lands Committee of the Corporation of London to forward two blocks of Portland stone from the structure of the old Temple Bar Monument for use in the new Temple Bar Lodge. These stones were gratefully accepted and formed into ashlars for use in the lodge. Smaller pieces of stone were then presented to each of the founder members as a memento of the old Temple Bar Monument from which the new lodge had taken its name. Sadly, sometime during the long history of the lodge, the original ashlars were lost and the dismantling of the Temple Bar in 2004 gave the lodge an opportunity to replace them. They contacted the stonemasons working on the project to see if they would be able to help. Having obtained approval from the City Architect, the stonemasons of the Cathedral Works Organisation who were working on the Temple Bar cut two new ashlars to replace those that had been lost. They were collected from Gary Collings, Site Manager of the Cathedral Works Organisation, by W Bro A. D. Gill in August 2004 and presented to the Worshipful Master W Bro Chris Hay and the brethren of the Temple Bar Lodge at their regular meeting on Tuesday 26 October 2004.

St Vedast-alias-Foster has a rather subtle steeple. LZ

STOP 18. Wren Churches

DIRECTIONS: On your right are the gates entering the north side of St Paul's Churchyard. Walk through to the exit at the other end. Cross to the opposite (east) side of New Change. Cross again, on your left, to the traffic island in the centre of Cheapside opposite Foster Lane. **STOP (18)** on the traffic island.

Historical Notes: Wren's Churches

The Great Fire of 1666 destroyed two-thirds of the City and a total of more than eighty city churches. Sir Christopher Wren was the architect chosen to rebuild fifty-one of those churches including St Paul's Cathedral. His master plan in rebuilding the churches took into account the importance and presence of St Paul's. He thus created an overall panorama of the City skyline, with dozens of steeples that appear to be there to decorate and emphasise the majesty of St Paul's itself. It is a sad reflection on human nature that the Second World War again destroyed so much and today just thirty-eight of the original ninety-seven pre-fire churches survive in the Square Mile. From this vantage point where you now stand a total of six of Wren churches are in view. It is symbolic that the foundation stones for many of the City churches were taken from the huge pile of rubble created when old St Paul's Cathedral was destroyed in 1666. St Paul's itself is flanked by the onion-shaped fibreglass steeple of St Augustine-with-St Faith (1680–87). The church was destroyed in 1941 and when rebuilt formed part of St Paul's Choir School. The surviving tower and steeple were rebuilt to Wren's original design. Turning to your left in an anti-clockwise direction, you will see the most famous of all London churches, St Mary-le-Bow (1670–83), which was gutted in 1941. The original distinctive steeple is classically by Wren. Here are contained the bells which make any person born within their sound a true London 'Cockney'.

Wren created an overall panorama of the City skyline. Guildhall

As you turn round, with your back to St Paul's, you face the distinctive Portland stone church of St Vedast-alias-Foster (1695-1700) with its rather subtle steeple, which changes dramatically as you walk across the front of the church. Agatha Christie was a parishioner and regular attendant. Further to the west is the prominent surviving tower of Christ Church, Newgate Street (1677–91) on the site of the Franciscan Greyfriars. Until 1902 Christ's Hospital, the school used by the 'Bluecoat Boys', stood here. Just beyond Christ Church is the sixth and last of the churches in view. St Sepulchre-without-Newgate, also known as the Church of the Holy Sepulchre, was not a Wren Church. It is one of the few City churches that survived the Great Fire and remains the largest parish church in the Square Mile. Its strategic position opposite the Old Bailey and the old Newgate prison has closely associated the church with condemned criminals, famously its bells ringing at 8.00am on those mornings when the condemned were put to death.

The calm and peace of the quaint gardens and courtyards of the City churches are in stark contrast to the surrounding noisy and busy daily life outside. Sadly, however, they are not always open. At the weekend the City streets are all but deserted and it is rather ironic that many churches are closed on Sunday. A few, dedicated to specific minority communities, enjoy full activity: the Orthodox Romanians are regular attendants at St Dunstan-in-the-West and the Filipinos frequent and enliven St Margaret Pattens. St Benet, Paul's Wharf, is dedicated to the Welsh community and the German Lutherans have traditionally and for a long time been closely associated with St Anne and St Agnes. St Bartholomew the Great and St Giles' Cripplegate serve the Barbican, which is the largest City residential complex, with some four thousand inhabitants. Today a group named 'Friends of the City Churches' does a great deal of voluntary work to ensure the survival and prosperity of the historic churches of the City.

Of Masonic Interest:
Was Wren a Freemason?

The general consensus is that had Sir Christopher Wren been a Freemason, as we understand the term today, there would have been unambiguous evidence of his membership of the Craft. As it is, those who promulgate his Masonic affiliation use evidence at times questionable. Wren was a member of the Worshipful Company of Masons, the ancient City Livery Company, but that is a far cry from his supposed initiation into a speculative Craft lodge.

Sir Christopher Wren, a gifted mathematician, scientist and architect, was born in East Knoyle, Wiltshire on 20 October 1632 and died 25 February 1723. He was a founding member of the Royal Society and is most famous for St. Paul's Cathedral, the building of which he personally oversaw between 1675 and 1710. Reports of his Masonic membership have arisen from various documents such as the records in the Royal Society archives, which

Sir Christopher Wren, mathematician, scientist and architect. Guildhall

state 'Bro. Christopher Wren was adopted into the Fraternity of Accepted Masons on May 18, 1691'. The word 'adopted' in this instance needs interpretation and there is no contemporary Masonic record of Wren's association with the Craft. The only oft-quoted source is a note made by John Aubrey (1626–1697), a non-Mason, on the manuscript of his book *Natural History of Wiltshire*, now in the Ashmolean Museum in Oxford, which reads:

> '. . . about Henry the Third's time, the Pope gave a bull or patents to a company of Italian Freemasons, to travel up and down all Europe to build churches. From those are derived the Fraternity of adopted masons.... The manner of their adoption is very formal and with an oath of secrecy.'

On the opposite sheet of the manuscript is an additional handwritten annotation reading:

> '1691 . . . this day, May the 18th, being Monday after Rogation Sunday is a great convention at St. Paul's Church of the Fraternity of the adopted masons, where Sir Christopher Wren is to be adopted a brother, and Sir Henry Goodric of the Tower, and divers others . . .'

Aubrey was prone to recount hearsay and admits that this statement was made to him by William Dugdale, an antiquarian and Ashmole's father-in-law. Whilst clearly some event of consequence took place in 1691 at St Paul's Cathedral there is no evidence that Sir Christopher Wren, at the mature age of 60, was initiated into the Craft. There is, however, a lasting tradition in the Lodge of Antiquity No 2 that Sir Christopher Wren was Master of the lodge. In *Records of the Lodge of Antiquity*, W. H. Rylands (1928) mentions 'Notes purporting to be either the original or extracts from an old minute book. The writing . . . could not have been written earlier than 1763'. This precludes the authority of a contemporary record. The third minutes of the lodge dated 18 March 1722, state:

'Several vestiges of the Old time were laid before the Lodge, particularly the Old Mallet used at laying the foundation stone of St. Paul's Cathedral . . . the Mallet ordered to be preserved in the Lodge as a Curiosity.'

The mallet is still preserved. A later entry of the meeting at the Queen's Arms on 26 July 1729 stating: 'Bro^r. Wren. Master', is thankfully undisputed and refers to Wren's son Christopher. Sir Christopher Wren himself, in his extensive writings, mentions Freemasonry but once in *The Architectonic Account of Salisbury Cathedral* when he states:

'The Italians, and with them French, Germans and Flemings, joined into a Fraternity of Architects, procuring Papal Bulls for their Encouragement and particular privileges: they styled themselves Freemasons and ranged from one Nation to another.'

He would surely have had more to say on the subject of Freemasonry had he patronised the Craft.

STOP 19. Saddlers' Hall

DIRECTIONS: Cross the street and walk straight ahead into Foster Lane. Past the church turn right into the tiny alleyway named Priest's Court. Walk through until you reach the large barred brick 'windows' on your right, beyond which you can see the front entrance to Saddlers' Hall. **STOP (19).**

Historical Notes: **Saddlers' Hall**
When first built at the end of the 14th century on this same site, Saddlers' Hall faced an open space looking towards Foster Lane. It was only at a later date that the church blocking the view was erected. Following the fire of 1666 the Hall was rebuilt keeping the front entrance to the hall in its original position, which now appears to be behind the building. The

entrance from Gutter Lane is through gates and a passage that leads to the main doors on the east side. Following a second fire in 1815, the building was again gutted by enemy fire in 1940 and this present building, by the architect L. Sylvester Sullivan, was completed in 1958. Through the first-floor windows facing Gutter Lane, the glistening chandeliers can often be seen. They are situated in the main dining hall and are an indication of the plush and rich interior of all Livery Halls. At the time of writing only thirty-nine of the one hundred and seven City Livery Companies have their own dedicated halls, which are used by the remaining Companies for their functions. The Worshipful Company of Saddlers is one of the older Liveries and is thought to descend from Anglo-Saxon predecessors. It received its first charter in 1272 and was incorporated in 1395, listed number 25 in seniority. Today the Company dedicates its charitable activity towards saddlery and riding in its many manifestations. It was, for instance, instrumental in supporting the British equestrian team at the Athens Olympic Games in 2004.

Of Masonic Interest:
The Structure of the Craft
One cannot emphasise sufficiently the need to differentiate clearly between us Freemasons, inadequately but effectively known as 'speculative' masons, and the working stonemason who makes his living from his trade, no less inadequately referred to as an 'operative' mason. A viable theory on the origins of 'speculative' Freemasonry is that it developed over the centuries along two parallel lines, namely form and content. Whilst the form has remained reasonably constant, it is the content that has evolved through umpteen processes leading to our present practices. But what is the origin of the form, the structure of Freemasonry that, since its organised inception in 1717, has not changed an iota?

The front entrance to Saddlers' Hall. LZ

The government of the Craft is clear and reasonably simple. We are individual members of private lodges duly registered in our Grand Lodge and led by Grand Officers with the Grand Master at our head. There is a striking similarity in this simplified representation of the administration of the Craft to the structure of the City of London. The latter can also be described as individual Liverymen, members of City Livery Companies duly registered in Guildhall and led by Aldermen of the City with the Lord Mayor at their head. The analogy can be taken further. The Livery companies consist of a Master, two Wardens and a Court of Assistants who conduct the Livery business. Every liveryman on his being made a member declares that he 'will conceal and not disclose . . . all the lawful secrets of the said art or mistery' (sic) of his particular trade. In earlier times Livery Company meetings took place in taverns and coffee houses and today they are conducted in one of the thirty-nine Livery Halls. The *raison d'être* of a Livery Company is charitable deeds with a strong emphasis on social activities, which revolve around festive dinners. The parallels are inescapable as is the one major difference. Whilst our lost origins as 'speculative' masons barely trace back to the early 17th century, the recorded history of the City, as a corporate identity, is in evidence in the Charter granted by William I in 1067, now housed in the City of London Records Office. This document recognises the rights of the City of London, expressing goodwill to 'all citizens, French and English' and confirming 'laws and customs as they were in King Edward's time'.

Enter the Guildhall Yard through the gates to the left of St Lawrence Jewry. LZ

STOP 20. Guildhall

DIRECTIONS: Walk left at Gutter Lane past Goldsmiths' Hall, then past Carey Lane and turn right into Gresham Street. Straight ahead the church of St Lawrence Jewry is in view. Walk towards it past Wood Street and enter the Guildhall Yard through the gates to left of the church at Aldermanbury. **STOP (20)** in the middle of the courtyard.

Historical Notes:
Guildhall and St Lawrence Jewry

It has often been said that this spot is the very heart and soul of the City, as it has been since 1128 or earlier. There is a wonderful contrast of architecture and history in the buildings that surround the yard. The 15th century Guildhall with its original 1411 walls on either side is in stark contrast to the new Guildhall Art Gallery, completed only in 1998 by Richard Gilbert Scott. As if to link the two, George Dance the Younger's white and prominent Hindu-Gothic porch decorates the entrance to the Guildhall.

The strange angle at which St Lawrence Jewry stands has been explained by the discovery in 1987 of the Roman gladiatorial arena on this site. It seems that the church was positioned to accommodate it. A mini-coliseum of some kind was known to have been erected by the Romans in the vicinity of the military fort of what is now the modern Barbican complex. The arena was discovered only when the excavations for the Art Gallery began. A dedicated and beautiful display of the archaeological dig is accessible to the public on the lower floor of the Art Gallery during opening hours. The 12th century church dedicated to St Lawrence, the martyr roasted alive over an open gridiron in the 3rd century, is commemorated by the weather vane

Guildhall . . . the very heart and soul of the City. LZ

recalling his martyrdom. The appellation 'Jewry' is a reminder of the presence of the Jewish community in this area until their expulsion by Edward I in 1290.

The church was destroyed in the fire of 1666 and rebuilt by Wren, being completed in 1687. It was again badly gutted on 29 December 1940 and restored to its present state in 1957 by Cecil Brown. The white interior with its gold leaf and chandeliers is spectacular. St Lawrence Jewry is the official church of the City of London and many of the formal services preceding events in the Guildhall are held here in the presence of the Lord Mayor and his whole retinue.

There is documentary evidence of a Guildhall in this area dated, as mentioned, 1128. The word 'guildhall' is derived from the Anglo-Saxon *gild* meaning 'payment' and it is thought that this was the tax collection point for the medieval citizens of London. The building survived both the Great Fire of London and the Blitz and is the only secular stone structure still standing in the City from before 1666.

The striking polygonal building to the west of the yard is the Alderman's Court, in front of the City of London's administrative buildings. Sir Giles Gilbert Scott, father of the architect of the Gallery, restored the whole site between 1955 and 1958. The Guildhall continues today as the centre of the City government, as it has since the Middle Ages. Major state and civic banquets are hosted by the Lord Mayor in the stupendous Great Hall with its splendid stained glass windows: the third largest civic hall in England. Through the centuries royalty and statesmen from around the world have been, and still are, entertained here. It has always been the venue for meetings of the Court of Common Council, the City of London's elected assembly. Many City ceremonies are performed here, ranging from the formal admission into office of the new Lord Mayor in November each year in the quaint 'Silent Ceremony', to the presentation of the Honorary Freedom of the City to dignitaries. The Great Hall has several monuments to national heroes including Admiral Lord Nelson, the Duke of Wellington and Sir Winston Churchill. Beneath the Guildhall lie the largest medieval crypts in London, occasionally used as banqueting and dining halls and hosting a number of City-associated Masonic lodges.

The polygonal Alderman's Court. LZ

St Lawrence's martyrdom is commemorated by the weather vane. LZ

Museum Notes: Guildhall Art Gallery

A Guildhall Art Gallery was first established in 1885 and the present building, formally opened in 1999, is the culmination of a century of effort to have a dedicated home for the City of London's substantial and important art collection. It houses and displays works of art commissioned and purchased since 1670. The Gallery and the Roman Amphitheatre are open Monday to Saturday from 10.00am to 5.00pm and on Sundays from 12.00 noon to 4.00pm. Admission costs £2.50 for adults and £1.00 concession; free for children under 16; also free every day after 3.30pm and all day Friday. Further information can be obtained by calling 020 7332 3700.

The passage named Guildhall Buildings is on the south side of the Art Gallery. LZ

STOP 21. Mason's Avenue

DIRECTIONS: Exit Guildhall Yard from the west along the passage named Guildhall Buildings on the south side of the Art Gallery. Turn left at Basinghall Street and the first passage entrance on your right is Masons Avenue.

STOP (21) at No 12-14, the Select Trust Building, some twenty yards into the alleyway. Note the large stained glass windows with the repeat Masonic design pattern. Just below, the gilt inscription engraved into the wall reads:

> *On This Site Stood*
> *The Hall Of The*
> *Worshipful*
> *Company*
> *Of Masons*
> *A 1463 – 1865 D*

Of Masonic Interest:
Worshipful Company of Masons

This site was the one-time home of the Guild of Stone Masons with which our Craft is so often mistakenly confused. The Company of Masons was formed, as were all other trade guilds, with the object of regulating the craft of their particular trade, stonemasonry in this instance, ensuring that high standards were maintained and protecting the consumer whilst rewarding the worker. The earliest available records of the Masons' Company are from 1356. In 1472 it received a Grant of Arms but had to wait a further two centuries before being formally incorporated in 1677 by a Royal Charter from Charles II. This was the period following the Great Fire of 1666 when the rebuilding of London necessitated an influx of foreign stonemasons, which in turn began to erode the control and power

Mason's Avenue. LZ

of the Company. The Charter allowed it to survive. Many notable buildings are accredited to the workmanship of the distinguished members of the Company. Thomas and Edward Strong, both Masters of the Company, were the senior stonemasons under Sir Christopher Wren during the building of St. Paul's Cathedral, undoubtedly the most famous building undertaken by the Company. The Company's own Hall was situated here close to the Guildhall. It was sold in 1865 and the inscription quoted above is all that remains of the building. As with other Livery Companies of the City of London, a Court of Assistants governs the membership of 125 Liverymen who, in this Company, are mostly connected with the construction industry. They are led by an annually elected Master and two Wardens and administered by an appointed Clerk. The activities of the Company are directed towards furthering the craft of stonemasonry and supporting related charities.

It is worth repeating that the London Company of Masons has no connection with our Craft. It is also true, however, that twenty-one Livery Companies have an associated Masonic lodge consisting exclusively of members of that particular Livery. On the other hand, there is also an element of reluctance amongst some Liverymen to show or admit any association between their Livery Company and Freemasonry. This is probably due to fears that the adverse publicity that Freemasonry has at times attracted may inadvertently taint the image of the Livery Companies.

The gilt inscription engraved into the wall of the Select Trust Building, Masons Avenue. LZ

Cheapside, with the famous St Mary-le-Bow Church. LZ

STOP 22. Cheapside

DIRECTIONS: Continue to the end of Mason's Avenue and turn right into Coleman Street. Cross Gresham Street and walk down Old Jewry, past Frederick's Place until you reach the crossroads where Cheapside meets Poultry. **STOP (22)**. To your right is Cheapside with the famous St Mary-le-Bow Church in view. To your left Poultry leads to the Bank of England.

Historical Notes: **Cheapside**

Poultry, where you stand, is the final extension of Cheapside, which runs from St Paul's to the Mansion House.

This was the 'Oxford Street' of the olden days. It was the greatest thoroughfare and shopping centre of the medieval city, with several tiered shops and homes on either side of the wide and long street. The original market was called Chepe or West Cheaping, as distinct from Eastcheap further south by London Bridge. The street was inhabited on the west by the Mercers and on the east by the Grocers, the two most senior Livery Companies. The alleyways in between were filled with taverns and inns. At the time of the fire in 1666, whilst the bankers of Lombard Street, within a stone's throw to the north, were intent on getting their gold

out, the vast majority of the shop owners in Cheapside saw their wooden structures burn to the ground in front of their eyes. Between the hours of midday and six o'clock in the evening of Sunday 2 September, the whole street simply disappeared. By dusk the Thames could be seen from where you stand at the top of Cheapside, for the first time since Roman days. Such devastation was not to be seen again until the German Blitz in 1940, which though horrendous did not match the damage caused by the fire in 1666.

Of Masonic Interest:
Thomas a Becket

My friend and colleague David Keeble Rees reminds me that Thomas a Becket was born in Ironmonger Lane (there is a plaque on the corner wall) and there was a Chapel of St Thomas of Acon near here until it was bombed in World War 2. All that remains is the recumbent statue of the Virgin Mary which lies in the entrance of the Mercers' Chapel now occupying the site. The (Masonic) Order of St Thomas of Acon is a Commemorative Order, with some 2,000 members throughout the world. They make a pilgrimage to Canterbury Cathedral in November every year, to hold a private service in the Crypt.

Cheapside was the 'Oxford Street' of the olden days. Guildhall

STOP 23. Mansion House

DIRECTIONS: Turn left along Cheapside, now named Poultry, to the main junction and **STOP (23)** at the railings to Bank Underground station. The Mansion House on the opposite side, as you will see, dominates the junction.

Though you are facing what was once the main entrance to the building, the volume of traffic necessitated its closure at the front. The entrance is now situated in Walbrook on the west side of Mansion House Place.

Historical Notes: **Mansion House**
The Mansion House is the home of the Lord Mayor of the City of London for the one year that he or she serves as Mayor. Since the election of Henry Fitz-Ailwyn as the first Mayor in 1189, the duties of the Mayor have involved the protection of the City's interests and the international promotion of trade for the City. This role of the Lord Mayor – who must be distinguished from the Mayor of London (Mr Ken Livingstone at the time of writing) — has become more sophisticated, though less powerful, over the centuries but has not changed in essence. The Lord Mayor entertains personalities and dignitaries, often on behalf of the monarch, and travels widely to promote the City. Traditionally the entertaining takes place in the Great Hall of the Guildhall or, often, in the Mayor's private residence, the Mansion House. A purpose-built home for the Mayor was first considered in 1666, following the Great Fire. It took an additional 70 years, however, finally to appoint George Dance the Elder (1695–1768), City Surveyor and Architect, to build what is now one of the grandest surviving Georgian town palaces in London. Although the first stone was laid in

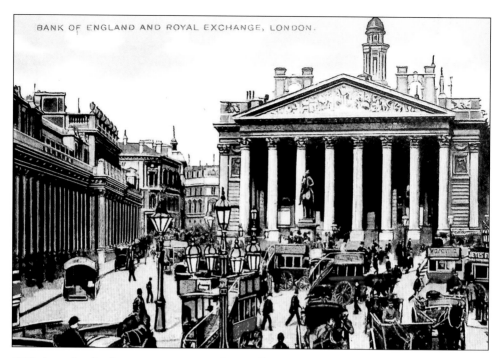

BANK OF ENGLAND AND ROYAL EXCHANGE, LONDON.

The quantity of traffic necessitated the closure of the main entrance at the front. DP

1739, it took a further 14 years to complete at a total cost of £70,000. Sir Crispin Gascoigne, Lord Mayor in 1752, impatient and unwilling to wait, was the first to take up residence, before the building was completed. The magnificent interior of the Mansion House has elaborate plasterwork and carved timber ornament.

It is ideally suited to host large ceremonial entertainments and banquets. It was originally built around a central courtyard, which was roofed over in 1794 and which now provides a large reception area. It also contained a cellar and cells for prisoners, who were held in the daytime when the Mansion House served as the Lord Mayor's magistrate court. The servants' quarters and the kitchens area are situated on the ground floor. The first floor comprises offices, dining and reception rooms and includes the famous and magnificent Egyptian Hall, so named because its giant columns replicate the dining halls used in Egypt in Roman times. The second floor has a gallery, which opens into the Egyptian room and is used for dancing and music recitals. The private chambers of the Lord Mayor and Lady Mayoress are situated on the third floor. Important and impressive classical paintings decorate the walls throughout the building. Notwithstanding extensive repair programmes over the years, the Mansion House has retained its original character and allows the Lord Mayor to represent the City in an impressive and appropriate style.

Museum Notes: **The Mansion House**

The Mansion House is open by appointment only for visits by organised groups (minimum 15 people, maximum 40). Applications can be made in writing to the Principal Assistant, Mansion House, London EC4N 8BH.

Of Masonic Interest: **Mayors as Masons**

The Egyptian Hall is suitable for large banquets. YB

There are many hundreds of Freemasons among the 24,000 Liverymen; 21 of the Livery Companies have their own Masonic lodges. There are also a number of City-orientated Masonic lodges such as the City of London Installed Masters Lodge and the City Livery Lodge, consisting exclusively of Liverymen whose Companies do not have their own Masonic lodge. Over the last century many Lord Mayors, Sheriffs and other City officials have been active Freemasons. In 1905 the Guildhall Lodge No 3116 was consecrated with the Lord Mayor for that year, RW Bro Col Sir Walter Vaughan Morgan as the first Worshipful Master of the lodge. Since that date a total of 71 Lord Mayors of the City have been Masters and at the time of writing Alderman Bro David Brewer, Lord Mayor, is also Master of the Guildhall Lodge. The lodge was formed with a view to bringing together City officials and on special occasions meets at the Ballroom in the Mansion House, the home of the Lord Mayor.

STOP 24. The Royal Exchange

DIRECTIONS: Cross Prince's Street and Threadneedle Street to your right making your way to the island, the eastern end of which is dominated by the massive portico with eight Corinthian columns and steps leading to the entrance of the Royal Exchange. **STOP (24)** in front of the steps next to the memorial, by Sir Aston Webb, to the London servicemen who lost their lives in the two World Wars.

Historical Notes: **The Royal Exchange**

The Royal Exchange is situated at the junction of Threadneedle Street and Cornhill. Nearby is Lombard Street, the medieval heart of the street market. It was not a comfortable way to trade daily in the open air at the mercy of passers-by and the elements. Thus the proposal of Sir Richard Gresham, Lord Mayor in 1537, to build an Exchange was most welcome.

The eight Corinthian columns at the entrance of the Royal Exchange. LZ

As a successful Mercer and trader in the Low Countries in particular, Richard Gresham liked the concept he witnessed in Antwerp of a commercial Exchange in whose precincts businessmen could trade safely and legally. It was his son, however, who brought the project to fruition. Sir Thomas Gresham (1518–1579) was the King's Merchant in Antwerp, which made him English Ambassador to Europe, and on his father's death in 1544 he moved to Lombard Street. From here, following the death of his only son Richard at the age of 10 in 1564, he dedicated himself to the erection of a London Exchange. He personally financed the whole building and laid the foundation stone on 7 June 1566. The Exchange was opened on the present site in November 1567. In January 1570, following a tour of the bourse, Queen Elizabeth I gave the enterprise her blessing, it thus becoming the Royal Exchange.

Trade within the quadrangular covered court, which was surrounded by colonnades, was active and dynamic. Statues of the monarchs decorated the whole area and the upper floors of the four-storey building,

which very much resembled the Bourse in Antwerp and Venice, had shops run by apothecaries, booksellers and goldsmiths, all of whom prospered. Thomas Gresham's crest, the grasshopper, is prevalent throughout the building, inside and out. On his death Gresham bequeathed the Royal Exchange to the Mercers' Company and to the Corporation of London. Sadly, as with so many other buildings in the City, the Royal Exchange burnt to the ground in 1666. It was rebuilt by the City surveyor, Edward Jarman, and opened its doors on 28 September 1669, a year after his death. Jarman was well known as the architect who rebuilt many of the City Livery Halls after the Great Fire. A second catastrophic fire, probably started in the Lloyd's premises in the building, began on 10 January 1838 and caused huge damage. The third bourse on the same site, the current building by Sir William Tite (1798–1873), was opened on 28 October 1844 by Queen Victoria to whom a

Businessmen could trade safely and legally.

Long-standing City traditions continue. Guildhall

monument by T. G. Lough was erected and placed in the centre of the quadrangle until its removal in 1896. By this time many of the trading organisations had moved out, initially to coffee houses to trade in dedicated groups before finally moving to custom-built premises. A few, however, remained within the Exchange precincts on a long-term basis: the Gresham Lecture room and The Lord Mayor's Court Office as well as the East India Company being prime examples. To this day the headquarters of the Guardian Royal Exchange Assurance Group is on the premises.

In 1939 the Royal Exchange ceased the functions for which it was created. Now sophisticated boutiques and restaurants follow in the footsteps of their ancestral shops and eating houses of 1567. There are, here and there, reminders of those days. The wall paintings of scenes of London's history are by Lord Leighton and other famous artists. There is even a surviving fragment of the original Turkish pavement from the time of the first hall.

Most importantly, long-standing City traditions continue: the new sovereign is proclaimed from the steps outside the Royal Exchange, as is the Dissolution of Parliament. These ceremonies have taken place from this very same spot for centuries.

STOP 25. Bank of England

DIRECTIONS: Pivot to your left. STOP (25). From this vantage point outside the Royal Exchange you have a view of the main entrance to the Bank of England from the south. It is situated on Threadneedle Street, which gives the Bank its well-known nickname: 'The Old Lady of Threadneedle Street'.

Historical Notes: The Bank of England

The most prominent architectural aspect of the Bank of England building is the clear distinction between the elongated screen wall along the front and the elevation beyond it.

Sir John Soane (1753–1837), the Bank's third architect, spent 45 years completing the enclosure of the quadrangle with his windowless wall in 1833, the year of his retirement. The Bank's boundaries have not altered since then, covering an area of three and a half acres. The elevation you can see beyond the wall was built relatively recently, between 1925 and 1939, by Sir Herbert Baker (1862–1946). It rises seven levels above ground and has three below. The wall is all that survives from John Soane's building. The Bank of England has been on this same site since 1734 and in this overall area since its inception in 1694. Prior to that date, from early medieval times this was the heart of the banking community. Signs hung from the buildings indicating the presence of bankers from all over the world. The nearby Lombard Street takes its name from the bankers from Lombardy in northern Italy. They arrived in England at the end of the 13th century to replace the Jews who had been expelled by Edward I in 1290 and it was their money that financed the many wars waged by the various monarchs. It also subsidised the King's lavish lifestyle in Whitehall and the Tower of London. When the Great Fire of London broke out in 1666, the bankers were most concerned with the preservation of their gold coins, which they moved out of the City to safety. It was this same gold which financed the rebuilding of the City after the fire. In 1693, five years into the reign of William and Mary, William Paterson (1658-1719), supported by his influential colleague Michael Godfrey, both active City merchants, proposed a public loan to the Government with funds raised from the citizens of London. The plan was to establish a national bank whose share capital would be the source for Government funding. It was a timely proposition. There were great trading possibilities in Europe in particular and the King needed to finance the war against France. Public finances had been weak for some years and the monetary system as a whole was in disarray. A national bank would

The main entrance to the Bank of England. LZ

POLITICAL-RAVISHMENT, ─ or, ─ The Old Lady of Threadneedle-Street in danger!

'The Old Lady of Threadneedle Street.' Guildhall

secure the mobilisation of the nation's resources. The proposal was accepted and an astounding total of £1,200,000 was raised within 11 short days. Parliament passed the Tunnage Act in July 1694, which guaranteed the 1,268 subscribers an 8% return on their investment. On 27 July 1694, The Company of the Bank of England was formed by Royal Charter and Sir John Houblon (1632–1711) was appointed its first Governor.

The Bank began its life by renting premises at the Mercers' Hall, situated in Cheapside, and a year later moved to a more spacious area at the Grocers' Hall in Prince's Street. It finally reached its present location in Threadneedle Street, which had been the site of Houblon's private residence, in 1734. The building by George Sampson (d.1764), Clerk of Works at the Tower of London, was the first purpose-built bank in the British Isles. The authorities continued to acquire neighbouring premises and land until the whole of the island it now occupies had been secured. Simultaneously the Bank consolidated its standing and its Charter was renewed in 1781.

From the start, the Bank of England acted as the Government's banker and debt manager. It made loans to finance peacetime spending as well as funding ongoing wars. It was also active as a commercial bank, taking deposits and issuing notes. By the end of the 18th century the Government's excessive borrowings led to what became known as the National Debt: that is, the amounts due from the Government to the Bank of England. As trade became more sophisticated, more restrictions were placed on the Bank of England's financial activities. The Bank Charter Act of 1844, on the one hand granted a monopoly to the Bank of England to issue notes, on the other it tied the Bank's note issues to its gold reserves. It also required the Bank to keep note issue records and accounts separate from its other banking activities. In more recent times, many of the financial crises of the 19th century were averted by the Bank of England's intervention. With the outbreak of the First World War and the huge increase in the National Debt it was again the Bank of England that helped manage Government borrowing and control inflationary tendencies and pressures. Following the decision in 1931 to leave the Gold Standard, which England had adhered to since 1816, all the gold and foreign exchange reserves were transferred to the Treasury. The management of the funds and bullion, however, remained, as it does to this day, in the hands of the Bank. Rather surprisingly, the Bank of England remained a private entity until the Parliament Act of 1946, when it was finally nationalised. Its duties did not change. A separate Royal Charter secured the continued existence of 'the Governor and Company of the Bank of England'. The 1979 and 1987 Banking Acts made the Bank of England 'The Bankers' Bank' with supervision rights over other banks. These responsibilities are now undertaken by the Financial Services Authority (FSA). The 1998 Bank of England Act made changes to the Bank's governing body, which now consists of the Governor, who is also Chairman of the Monetary Policy Committee, two Deputies and sixteen non-executive Directors appointed by the Crown on the advice of the Prime Minister.

Statistical records of City finances in recent years make staggering reading. The amount of foreign exchange turnover in the City exceeds five hundred billion US dollars *daily*, 48% of the global foreign equity market is centred in London and some 70% of all Eurobonds are traded in London. These are just three examples. No wonder the City of London, that one square mile, is the world's largest international financial centre.

Of Masonic Interest: Sir John Soane

Sir John Soane, undoubtedly the most prominent architect of his time, was also responsible for the rebuilding of Freemasons' Hall in Great Queen Street, shortly after the Union of 1813. He was a Freemason of high rank, Grand Superintendent of Works, which he achieved rather rapidly. When Soane was first approached by Grand Lodge in March 1813 to survey and value the premises adjoining Freemasons' Tavern in Great Queen Street, he was not a Freemason.

He had been, however, since 1776, well known to the Duke of Sussex, Grand Master of the 'Moderns'. The election of George III's son as Grand Master of the United Grand Lodge of England in 1813 brought Freemasonry into fashion and soon there was a requirement to expand the available space at Freemasons Tavern. It was at the Duke of Sussex's instigation that Soane was invited to become a mason and was offered the role of Grand Superintendent of Works. Soane's only exposure to Freemasonry was his admiration and respect for his tutor, Thomas Sandby (1721–1798), a founder member of the Royal Academy in 1768 and its first professor of architecture. Until his death in 1798, Sandby had been a senior member of the Grand Lodge of England. It was Sandby who had designed and built the original Freemasons Hall in 1775–1776 and it is probable that Soane felt proud to follow in the footsteps of his mentor. On 25 November 1813 an Emergency Lodge was convened at Freemasons' Hall and John Soane was initiated into Freemasonry, passed to a Fellowcraft and raised to the Sublime Degree of a Master Mason all in the course of the evening. In December 1813, following the formal inauguration of the United Grand Lodge of England with the Duke of Sussex as Grand Master, John Soane was among those named as Grand Officers for the ensuing year and he was formally appointed President of the Board of Works . . . speedy advancement by any standards!

Museum Notes

The Bank of England Museum was formally opened in 1988. The carefully arranged displays and re-creations are intended to detail the Bank's history whilst portraying the Bank as an evolving institution. The Museum is situated within the Bank itself with an entrance in Bartholomew Lane that leads the visitor into the reconstructed Bank Stock Office, designed in the late 18th century by Sir John Soane. It is open to the public Monday to Friday, 10.00am to 5.00pm and will accept bookings for tours from special interest groups. It is closed at weekends and on Public and Bank Holidays. Call the Museum on 020 7601 5545 and a recorded message will confirm the times and other details. Admission to the Museum is free of charge.

STOP 26. Monument to Wellington

DIRECTIONS: With your back to the Royal Exchange you have a view of the busiest road junction in the City. Seven streets — Threadneedle, Prince's, Poultry, Victoria, King William, Lombard and Cornhill — meet at the intersection facing the Mansion House. The proud and imposing equestrian monument to Wellington appears to be keeping a watchful eye on the animated activity.

Historical Notes: **Monument To Wellington**

Wellington is the only English hero to whom two equestrian statues have been erected in London. The other, formerly at Hyde Park Corner, is now at the Round Hill in Aldershot where it was placed in 1885. This large and beautiful equestrian bronze figure of Wellington on horseback stands on a granite pedestal and was cast in bronze entirely from cannons captured from the defeated French forces and brought back to England by Wellington himself. The famous sculptor, Sir Francis Legatt Chantrey (1781–1841) had only completed the preliminary model when he died and the

The proud and imposing equestrian monument to Wellington. LZ

work was taken over by his assistant Henry Weekes (1807–1877), who was later to become famous in his own right. It was completed in 1844, the year of the opening of the new Royal Exchange. Wellington himself was present at the unveiling, although this was a statue not to honour his military victories but in recognition of the help he had given the City Corporation in enabling a Bill to be passed to allow the rebuilding of London Bridge. The legend at the base of the monument states:

Erected June 1844
19 July 1838 The Court of Common Council of the City of London agreed to a contribution of £500 toward the cost of the above statue of the Duke of Wellington in appreciation of his efforts in assisting the passage of the London Bridge Approaches Act

The fact that there are neither saddle nor stirrups on the horse has been commented upon. Notwithstanding the many fanciful stories and anecdotes as to the reason, the simple fact is that the lack of stirrups is an early Roman symbolic representation of military authority and equestrian competence.

Of Masonic Interest:
Wellington as a Freemason

The eventful life of Arthur, Duke of Wellington, was evenly apportioned between a triumphant military career and a hardly less remarkable political one. He was also a Freemason and, for five years, a member of the lodge in Trim, Ireland, although never progressing beyond the first degree of Freemasonry. Arthur Wellesley was born in Dublin on 1 May 1769 and through the influence of his elder brother Richard was launched on a military career from an early age. In April 1790 Arthur was elected Member of Parliament for Trim, Ireland. He was 21 years old and his decision to be initiated into the family lodge on 7 December of the same year may have been influenced by political expediency. There is no doubt, however, of the intense involvement of his immediate family in the Craft. Both his father and his brother served as Masters of the Trim Lodge No 494 and they both reached the peak of their Masonic careers as Grand Masters of the Grand Lodge of Ireland. Garrett Wellesley, first Earl of Mornington, was proposed as a member of the lodge by one of its founders, John Boulger, and raised a Master Mason in July 1775. A year later he served as Worshipful Master of the lodge and was elected Grand Master of the Grand Lodge of Ireland, serving for one year, as was customary at that time, being succeeded by the Duke of Leinster in 1776. His eldest son, Richard, 3rd Baron and 2nd Earl of Mornington, was raised on 31 July 1781, having paid his late father's arrears and his own admission fee a few weeks earlier.

A year later he followed in the footsteps of the Right Honourable William Randall, Earl of Antrim (who also served as Grand Master of the *Antients* Grand Lodge of England) as the new Grand Master of Ireland. Wellington would no doubt have followed in their footsteps had time permitted him to pursue his Masonic career. There is no reason to suppose that the young Arthur was in any way disenchanted with the Craft. The lodge records show that on 7th December 1790 he paid his admittance fee of '£2 5s 6d'. He is here referred to as 'the Honorable Capt. Wesley'. A second entry on 26 June 1792 states 'Pd now in advance Br. Wesley 14s 1d'. The records continue to show several occasions on which his dues are paid, the last entry being on 8 September 1795. A further telling entry of his continued, even active, interest in lodge affairs is his part-purchase of an English lottery ticket on 16 February 1795 from the Treasurer of the lodge. The minutes for that date show that two English lottery tickets, which were the property of the only remaining seven regular Brethren of the lodge, cost £45 10s 0d and '. . . the members who subscribed and are entitled to benefit of the tickets purchased of part of their fifty pounds are . . . the Honorable A.Wesley . . .'

The logical conclusion that Arthur had intentions to progress in the Craft is supported by the words of Lord Combermere, Provincial Grand Master of Cheshire, at the death of Wellington. On 31 December 1852 *The Freemasons' Quarterly Magazine and Review* reported verbatim Lord Combermere's words addressed to the Brethren of the Province on 27 October of the same year:

'Perhaps it is not generally known that he (the Duke of Wellington) was a mason; he was made in Ireland; and often when in Spain, where Masonry was prohibited, in conversation (with Lord Combermere) he regretted repeatedly how sorry he was his military duties had prevented him taking the active part his feelings dictated.'

The Duke of Wellington . . . military hero, outstanding politician, Freemason . . . Guildhall

inscription on Peter Stuart Ney's tomb in the Third Creek Presbyterian Church in rural Rowan County, North Carolina, USA:

'In memory of Peter Stuart Ney, a native of France and soldier of the French Revolution under Napoleon Bonaparte, who departed this life Dec. 15, 1846, aged 77 years.'

Peter Stuart Ney, a schoolmaster, was buried there in 1846. His last words on his deathbed are reported to have been: 'By all that is holy, I am Marshal Ney of France!' It is interesting to note that the implication is that Peter Stuart Ney was born in 1769, the year of *Marshal* Ney's birth — as well as that of Wellington and Napoleon Bonaparte.

The Duke of Wellington stands out as England's greatest military hero and an outstanding politician. Circumstances did not allow him to pursue a Masonic career. It detracts little from the pride we take in the Wellesleys' membership of our ancient Craft.

There is one curious incident in which Wellington came face to face with his Masonic reputation. The French Marshal Michel Ney, who famously met his end during the 'White Terror' as a traitor and was executed by a firing squad on 7 December 1815 in a Paris public park, recognised Wellington as a fully-fledged Masonic brother. Marshal Ney, in a letter, appealed to Wellington 'as a Brother' to assist and save his life. Wellington was not in a position to intervene. Ney had been initiated in Le Trinosophes Lodge number 494 in Paris under the Grand Orient of France and a legend has persisted that the 'Bravest of the Brave', as he had been referred to by Napoleon, escaped execution with the help of French Freemasons and the Duke of Wellington. The legend is perpetuated by the

End of Walk

DIRECTIONS: You have now reached the end of the walk and you are conveniently situated for public transport to whichever part of London you wish to proceed. Surrounding you are several entrances to Bank Underground station, which is on both the Northern and Central Lines. In addition, a Docklands Light Railway line as well as the Waterloo and City Line run from the station to various destinations. The multitude of buses will take you in all directions. The final destination of each bus will appear on the display unit at each bus stop. Finally, do remember the City is only one square mile and, even though the walk may have taken the best part of two hours, your direct return route to Freemasons' Hall from here is just a 20-minute brisk walk.

Please join us on another City of London walk soon. Readers are invited to join the London Guide Tours for further exploration of the City.

SUMMARY OF THE WALK & MAP

A Walk in the City with Yasha Beresiner

STOP 1. Freemasons' Hall
See page 23 for Notes

Directions: The address of Freemasons' Hall is Great Queen Street, London WC2 and the switchboard telephone number is 020 7831 9811. Access is easy by Underground to Holborn Station on the Central and Piccadilly Lines. Exit onto Kingsway and turn left. The second street on your right, at the traffic lights where you can cross over safely, is Great Queen Street. The entrance to Freemasons' Hall is on the left past the Connaught Rooms.

STOP 2. Great Queen Street
See page 25 for Notes

Directions: Walk out of Freemasons' Hall onto Great Queen Street and turn right towards Kingsway, Holborn. STOP (2) is at the end of Great Queen Street at its intersection with Kingsway.

STOP 3. The Old Curiosity Shop
See page 25 for Notes

Directions: At the top of Great Queen Street cross Kingsway to the opposite side and turn right, walking south towards Aldwych. At Sardinia Street turn left and the first turning to your right is Portsmouth Street. A few yards along on your left is STOP (3), one of the oldest buildings extant in London: The Old Curiosity Shop.

STOP 4. Lincoln's Inn
See page 27 for Notes

Directions: Continue straight down Portsmouth Street, turn right into Portugal Street and immediately left into St Clement's Lane. At the end turn right into Grange Court. On your left is Clement's Inn Gate and steps leading down to the pedestrian path. This will take you out through the gate that leads to the Strand. STOP (4): you will be facing, on the traffic island opposite, the north wall of St Clement Danes Church in the Strand.

STOP 5. The Temple Bar Memorial
See page 29 for Notes

Directions: Turn left and walk in front of the Royal Courts of Justice to the second set of pedestrian lights. Cross to the south side and turn to face the street. STOP (5). Straight ahead, on the opposite side of the street, are the impressive white buildings you have just walked past: the Royal Courts of Justice and, rather imposing, in the middle of the street to your right is the Temple Bar Memorial surmounted by an enormous heraldic dragon.

STOP 6. The Devil Tavern
See page 35 for Notes

Directions: Walk a few yards to No 1 Fleet Street, now the home of the famous City bankers Messrs Child & Co. STOP (6). On the wall to the left of the main entrance is a blue plaque which reads *'Site of the Devil Tavern demolished 1787'*. From here you also have your first glimpse of Fleet Street running eastwards towards St Paul's Cathedral.

STOP 7. The Temple Area
See page 37 for Notes

Directions: Continue a few yards east along Fleet Street until you reach a stone gateway on your right, headed *'Middle Temple Lane — 1684'*. (The gates are closed at night and at weekends.) Enter the Temple area, bearing in mind that you are now on private property. Walk down the lane past Brick Court until you are in sight of the impressive Middle Temple Hall on your right. STOP (7) is in the middle of Fountain Court and gardens. This is where,

according to Shakespeare, the plucking of the red rose of Lancaster and the white rose of York led to the historic Wars of the Roses (1455–1485).

STOP 8. Temple Church
See page 40 for Notes

Directions: Cross over to Pump Court on your left and walk through the small archway towards the Lamb Building and up the steps into Temple Church Courtyard. STOP (8). You are now in the Inner Temple. Note the Pegasus winged horse

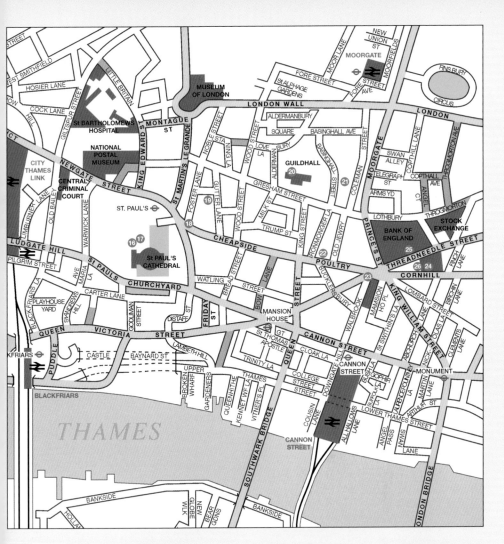

symbol decorating the walls of the buildings. Stand by the column, which has at the top a bronze statue by Nicola Hicks of two knights sharing a horse. It was completed and erected in 2000. Enter the church in your own time.

STOP 9. Prince Henry's Room
See page 44 for Notes

Directions: Exit Temple Church and turn sharply to your right. Leave the Inner Temple area by walking along the left-hand side (west) of the church past Dr Johnson's

Building. Note the exterior of the Norman gate entrance into Temple Church as you go past. Exit by the north end gateway back into Fleet Street, opposite Chancery Lane. STOP (9). The half-timber work of the gateway comprises Prince Henry's Room and the Pepys Museum above the gateway.

STOP 10. Mitre Tavern
See page 46 for Notes

Directions: Turn right along Fleet Street towards St Paul's and after about 50 yards further on stop at No 37 Fleet Street, now

'Mssrs. Hoare Bankers AD1672', immediately opposite St Dunstan in the West Church. STOP (10). On the wall by the entrance is another blue plaque, which reads *'Site of the Mitre Tavern'*.

STOP 11. Gough Square

See page 50 for Notes

Directions: Continue along Fleet Street to the second set of pedestrian lights and cross to the other side. Turn right towards St Paul's Cathedral and take the third lane on your left, following the signpost to Dr Johnson's House. Walk past the blue plaque on the wall until you reach Gough Square. STOP (11).

STOP 12. Cheshire Cheese Tavern

See page 53 for Notes

Directions: Walk through the archway to the left of the statue of Hodge, the cat, into Gunpowder Square. Wine Office Court faces you and extends to your right. Turn right towards the Cheshire Cheese sign visible less than 50 yards ahead. Wine Office Court derives its name from the tax offices situated here, where payment for wine and spirit licences was made in the 17th and 18th centuries. STOP (12) at the rails opposite the entrance to the Cheshire Cheese Tavern.

STOP 13. Fleet Street

See page 56 for Notes

Directions: Exit the Cheshire Cheese and turn left, leaving Wine Office Court and back onto Fleet Street. Turn left again and walk 200 yards to the Daily Express building at number 120-129 on the corner of Shoe Lane. STOP (13).

STOP 14. St Bride's Church

See page 59 for Notes

Directions: The little island in the middle of Fleet Street will help you cross to the other side. There is no pedestrian crossing at this point. Enter St Bride's Churchyard through St Bride's Avenue. Walk through the main gate into the courtyard. STOP (14).

STOP 15. Fleet River

See page 59 for Notes

Directions: Exit the gates of St Bride's Church and return to Fleet Street turning right towards St Paul's. Cross New Bridge Street at the lights and turn right towards Blackfriars Bridge. STOP (15) at the base of the steps at Pilgrim Street.

STOP 16. St Paul's and the Goose and Gridiron

See page 60 for Notes

Directions: Climb the steps and walk past Pageantmaster Court. Turn right at Ludgate Broadway and then left into Carter Lane. Walk to the top, passing the King's Wardrobe on your right and turn left into Dean's Court past the Bishop of London's Mansion. At the main road leading to Ludgate Hill, St Paul's Cathedral looms enormous and proud before you. Turn left to the crossing and make your way to the bottom step of St Paul's Cathedral. Follow the lowest step to your left until you reach the columns of Paternoster Square STOP (16). You stand at what was the entrance to the Goose and Gridiron Tavern. The plaque commemorating the formation of Grand Lodge in 1717 is on your right at the end of the row.

STOP 17. Return of the Temple Bar

See page 63 for Notes

Directions: A few yards from the plaque is the great gateway: the recently restored old Temple Bar. STOP (17).

STOP 18. Wren Churches
See page 65 for Notes

Directions: On your right are the gates leading to the north side of St Paul's Churchyard. Walk through to the exit at the other end. Cross to the opposite (east) side of New Change. Cross again, on your left, to the traffic island in the centre of Cheapside opposite Foster Lane. STOP (18) on the traffic island.

STOP 19. Saddlers' Hall
See page 68 for Notes

Directions: Cross the street and walk straight ahead into Foster Lane. Past the church on your right, turn right into a tiny alleyway named Priest's Court. Walk through until you reach the large barred brick 'windows' on your right, beyond which you can see the front entrance to Saddlers' Hall. STOP (19).

STOP 20. Guildhall
See page 70 for Notes

Directions: Turn left into Gutter Lane past Goldsmiths' Hall, pass Carey Lane on your left and turn right into Gresham Street. Straight ahead the church of St Lawrence Jewry is in view. Walk towards it past Wood Street and enter the Guildhall Yard through the gates to the left of the church at Aldermanbury. STOP (20) in the middle of the courtyard.

STOP 21. Masons Avenue
See page 73 for Notes

Directions: Exit Guildhall Yard from the west along the passage named Guildhall Buildings, on the south side of the Art Gallery. Turn left into Basinghall Street and the first passage entrance on your right is Mason's Avenue. STOP (21) at No 12-14, the Select Trust Building, some twenty yards into the alleyway. Note the large stained glass windows with the repeat Masonic design pattern. Just below, a gilt inscription engraved on the wall reads:

> *On This Site Stood*
> *The Hall Of The*
> *Worshipful*
> *Company*
> *Of Masons*
> *A 1463 – 1865 D*

STOP 22. Cheapside
See page 76 for Notes

Directions: Continue to the end of Mason's Avenue and turn right into Coleman Street. Cross Gresham Street and walk down Old Jewry, past Frederick's Place on your right, until you reach the point where Cheapside meets Poultry. STOP (22). To your right is Cheapside with the famous St Mary-le-Bow Church in view and to your left Poultry leads to the Bank of England.

STOP 23. Mansion House
See page 77 for Notes

Directions: Turn left along Cheapside, now named Poultry, to the main junction and STOP (23) at the railings to Bank Underground station. The Mansion House on the opposite side, as you will see, dominates the junction. Though you are facing what was once the main entrance, the volume of traffic necessitated its closure at the front of the building. The entrance is now situated on the west side of the building in Mansion House Place.

STOP 24. The Royal Exchange
See page 79 for Notes

Directions: Keeping to your left, cross Prince's Street and Threadneedle Street making your way onto the island, the eastern end of which is dominated by a massive portico with the eight Corinthian columns and steps leading to the entrance of the Royal Exchange. STOP (24) in front of the steps next to the memorial, by Sir Aston Webb, to the London servicemen who lost their lives in the two World Wars.

STOP 25. Bank of England
See page 82 for Notes

Directions: Pivot to your left. STOP (25). From this vantage point outside the Royal Exchange you have a view of the main entrance to the Bank of England from the south. It is situated on Threadneedle Street, which gives the Bank its well-known nickname: 'The Old Lady of Threadneedle Street'.

STOP 26. Monument to Wellington
See page 86 for Notes

Directions: With your back to the Royal Exchange you have a view of the busiest road junctions in the City. Seven streets — Threadneedle, Prince's, Poultry, Victoria, King William, Lombard and Cornhill — meet at the intersection facing the Mansion House. The proud and imposing equestrian monument to Wellington appears to be keeping a watchful eye on the animated activity.

End of Walk

Directions: You have now reached the end of the walk and are conveniently situated for public transport to whichever part of London you wish to proceed. Surrounding you are several entrances to Bank Underground station, which is on both the Northern and Central Lines. In addition, a Docklands Light Railway line as well as the Waterloo and City Line run from the station to various destinations. The multitude of buses will take you in all directions. The final destination of each bus will appear on the display unit at each bus stop. Finally, do remember the City is only one square mile and even though the walk may have taken the best part of two hours, your direct return route to Freemasons' Hall from here is just a 20-minute brisk walk.

Please join us on another City of London Walk soon.

INDEX

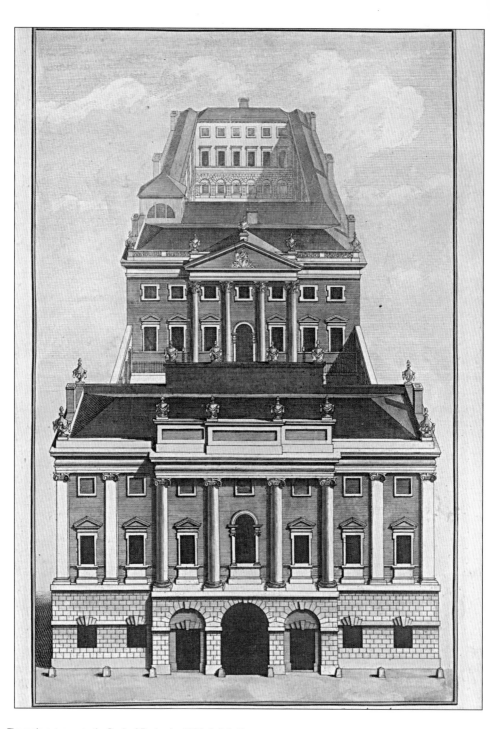

The main entrance to the Bank of England, c1780. Guildhall